Helping Across Cultures

Edited By
Gordon L. Lippitt and David S. Hoopes

Published by the International Consultants Foundation, 1978
Washington, D.C. and London, England

FOREWORD

Because of the importance and relevance of this subject, I am particularly glad to have been asked to write the foreword for such a worthwhile book. An understanding of, and ability to, help across cultures is increasingly vital within a country (as well as abroad) where there are new cultural mixes and rising expectations among minority groups.

Who better to write on "Helping Across Cultures" than Gordon Lippitt and David Hoopes? Both speak with immense authority and experience; that experience is complementary. Professor Lippitt (well known for his film series and management books on such related topics as "Visualizing Change" and "Organization Renewal") is an academic with a real (and all too rare) practical understanding of cross-cultural problems. It has been my privilege to see Gordon handling multi-national groups such as senior management of the World Health Organization. His co-editor, David Hoopes, is a specialist—perhaps the specialist—in the cross-cultural area. As founding Executive Secretary of the Society for Intercultural Education, Training and Research and President of the Intercultural Network, Inc., he has fostered nationally and internationally the study of intercultural communication and the development of cross-cultural training over a fifteen year period.

As the first chapter emphasizes, today, 'Multicultural Person' is as important—if not more important—than 'Multilingual Person'. People need to be able to communicate effectively with those of other cultures. Individuals working (and living) in different countries must become more culturally sensitive and cosmopolitan than ever before. Apart from the obvious need for people involved in international operations, an increasing number face cross-cultural problems at home where two, three or even more different cultural groups can be represented in a workforce.

Communication is difficult enough between those who share the same values, beliefs and expectations. The difficulties become acute when there are significant differences in these basic attitudes. Learning a language is never enough. Probably more lipservice is paid to the need for improving communication than any other topic. Yet, how many costly communication failures occur in organizations today? Not even lipservice is paid to cross-cultural communication:To my mind there is an emphatic gap in management development programmes, that important gap lies in the cross-cultural dimension.

Having worked as a consultant for the United Nations Secretariat and the Commission of the European Communities as well as in every Continent, I have seen only too clearly the need for helping across cultures. However, recognition of this need is often the biggest problem. This book makes a positive contribution to meeting that need.

2

In helping across cultures, are we doing it all wrong? When British managers go abroad, they are usually given an excellent briefing on the country concerned. But, surely the basic need is for them to have a real understanding of their own cultural norms, perceptions, stereotypes, values, etc. as the sound foundation for studying those of others.

This book will be extremely helpful to senior management and to international consultants. It will also be highly relevant to a much wider readership, especially all those concerned with human resource development world-wide.

Thomas J. Attwood
President
International Consultants Foundation
and Cargill, Attwood & Thomas Ltd.
London, England
August, 1978

TABLE OF CONTENTS

4

BOOK AUTHORS AND CONTRIBUTORS

Thomas Attwood, President
Cargill Attwood International
London, England

David S. Brown, Professor
George Washington, University
Washington, D.C. USA

David S. Hoopes (Co-editor), President
Intercultural Network, Inc.
Vermont, USA

Herman P. Hoplin, Management Consultant
Virginia, USA

Gordon L. Lippitt (Co-editor), Professor
George Washington University
Washington, D.C. USA

Peggy Lippitt, Board Member/Consultant
Human Resource Development Associate
Michigan, USA

Phyllis E. Lippitt, Vice President
Project Associates, Inc.
Maryland, USA

Ronald Lippitt, President
Human Resource Development Associate
Michigan, USA

Garld H. Malin, Director of Training
Department of Social Services
Regina, Canada

Richard D. Miller, President
R.D. Management Associates, Inc.
Virginia, USA

Leonard Nadler, Professor
George Washington University
Washington, D.C. USA

Zeace Nadler, Partner
Nadler Associates
Maryland, USA

E. Bruce Peters, President
International Sociotechnical Systems
Virginia, USA

William J. Reddin, President
International Publications, Ltd.
Bermuda

Eve Schindler-Rainman
Organization and Community Consultants
California, USA

Wilson L. Tilley, President
W.L. Tilley Associates
Connecticut, USA

CHAPTER ONE
Cross-Cultural Consultation—A Growing Need In Today's World
by Gordon Lippitt

One of the most difficult things for an individual, a group, an organization, a profession, or a nation to accomplish is the act of helping another human system without creating suspicion, hostility, or dependence. The ICF international work conference was convened for the purpose of exploring problems, and their causes and possible solutions, in increasing the effectiveness of giving and receiving help in cross-cultural settings.

Results today, especially in consultation from one country to another, depend more and more upon "people" skills between "helper" and "helpee." But problems inevitably occur when people of different cultures intermingle. Concepts and methods which are successful in one country can spell disaster in another. Cross-cultural compatibility and skills can make the vital difference between effective consulting performance and costly but avoidable failures. Such skills also can make the difference between apathy or hostility and constructive application. Those engaged in international consultation today need to be multi-cultural even more than they need to be multi-lingual.

In this era of worldwide problems, needs for technological and social applications in all countries, in multi-national corporations, in a multiplicity of international organizations, and especially in developing countries, are great. The need to improve the process of giving and receiving help is a key factor in economic and sociological interdependence. It is important to examine ways in which planned consultation can go beyond the exchange of experts, international "visits," or technical assistance.

For example, it is generally believed that the promotion of "understanding" is synonymous with the promotion of "good will." Research finds no grounds for this assumption. When the policies are right and understood, others may not like them or may consider them opposed to their own interests.

Nor should we assume that face-to-face meetings and personal association of peoples will necessarily engender sympathy and mutual accord. This idea somehow survives despite persistent reports of abrasive collisions between tourists and their foreign hosts, and despite the obvious fact that some nations which deal with one another constantly also have fought each other frequently.

Such broad assumptions are an inadequate base upon which to base cross-cultural consultation: for example, to expand the use of third country consultants or to spend limited resources. We must be more specifically concerned with the persons exchanged, what they do, and how they do it.

Cross-cultural consultation has become a process of interaction which occurs in many settings and among peoples of many different backgrounds and occupations. This kind of intensive interactional exchange brings with it both new problems and learning opportunities. When an individual goes abroad to study medicine or philosophy from a world-renowned master, there are few learning problems. The subject matter generally is considered a-cultural; it is not the specific property of any one nation or historical tradition. In the case of cross-cultural consultation, the situation is quite different. The objective is to make an impact upon a person, group, or organization in another culture. We need to view such a process from a perspective based upon anthropological knowledge of cultural exchange as well as upon psychological knowledge of the process of change. Consulting impact depends upon the conditions within client systems as well as the particular dynamics of the consulting relationship.

There are different ways in which the social, psychological, and cultural influence can affect the consulting experience in cross-cultural consultation. The willingness of clients to adjust and look at new ideas depends upon their past experience. The client and consultant both bring values and knowledge from their own countries, and if something new is to be acceptable to the client, it must be consistent with both. Application in one's home country of consultation learnings may be a problem. There is need for an effective understanding of the client's needs and of the reactions of those persons who will be affected by the consulting process. What is possible for the client to accept, and vice versa? Does the problem-solving which occurs during a consultation persist after the consultation is completed? How effective is consultation as a means of bringing about change? How important is it to develop "in-country" resources and other types of follow-up after the consultants return to their own countries? These are practical questions which need to be considered in evaluating cross-cultural consultation. Such questions should be asked in terms of present world trends, unmet needs in cross-cultural consultation, and the role of the professional in this important help-giving endeavor.

Major Trends in the International Field

The need for cross-cultural consultation is reflected in the multiplicity of crises in today's world. Let me review, quickly, some of the major forces at work in the current situation in order to help bring them into focus. I do this in the knowledge that there are no easy answers for developing effective consultation programs. We can, however, analyze what it is that we are now doing, and perhaps adapt and change to meet these changing times.

1. World-wide Growth of the Population

A listing of major problems in the world today might well begin with the population explosion, save perhaps for the danger of nuclear war. There has been so much talk about the explosion in numbers of people that those of us in countries where the rate of population growth is relatively slow are inclined to give up. "When are those people in India and China going to learn?" We say, in effect, and turn our eyes from what we consider to be *their* problem alone. Obviously, it is not solely their problem, as the front-page stories of our newspapers daily make clear. Is the population explosion a problem we can safely ignore? Can we afford not to think about consultation and education for birth control, and about its moral, psychological, and political implications? I think not.

Population growth is putting heavy pressure upon food supplies which are already short of meeting world needs; upon all of our public services; upon economic growth trends which in some cases are being arrested; and upon our professional skills and organizational capacity. A sharing of experience and expertise in these skills and this capacity is very much needed.

2. Continued Economic and Social Imbalance between Nations

Countries of the world are unequal in their resources and utilization of resources. The developing countries represent major geographical and population areas. The United Nations estimates that there are 4 billion people living in 126 underdeveloped areas throughout the world.

Among the characteristics of an underdeveloped country are widespread poverty, a lack of power and light, inadequate communications systems (roads, railroads, telephones, etc.), and insufficient government services. There are too few hospitals, schools, and institutions of higher learning. The majority of the people can neither read nor write. The banking system is rudimentary˙ and interest rates are unreasonably high. Major exports, frequently controlled by foreign companies, are raw materials of either an extraction type (tin, copper, oil) or cultivation type (rubber, coffee, etc.). In spite of these adverse conditions, there is always a small group of people in these areas who live in luxury.

What are the major needs of the underdeveloped areas? They are too numerous to list in detail, but three are: (1) to increase production, (2) to improve distribution of production, and (3) to stimulate in the people a favorable attitude toward change. Cross-cultural consultation is relevant today to meeting such needs and thus lessening the gap between developed and underdeveloped nations.

3. World Food Crisis

One of the great crises of the world is hunger and famine in Africa,

8

Latin America, and Asia. This crisis is imposing great burdens in countries which do not have the agricultural or economic experience to feed growing numbers of their own population. Further increases in population, combined with the need for more food, could convert this present crisis into a global catastrophe within our lifetime—unless the "have" nations quickly assist the "have not" countries to meet their basic need for food. The experience of agricultural consultants in Canada, Europe, the U.S.A. and other countries is needed to help confront the issue.

4. Increased Interdependency between Nations

It is a well-recognized fact that the world is now economically, geographically, and sociologically interdependent. The recognition that one country can learn much from another is a modern phenomenon. This provides the underlying foundation for the values of cross-national consultation. Every culture can contribute something to the knowledge and practices of another.

5. Increased Development of National Pride

There is increasing self-recognition in developing countries of their heritages, and a mounting pride of these peoples in their history. In struggling to improve their condition, it will be important—as they learn from others—that they also preserve their identity, their unique character. It will be necessary not only to help channel such pride, but to protect it, a key factor in cross-cultural consultation.

6. Increased Tempo of the Industrial Revolution

Economic imbalances still are hastening industrial revolution in the developing countries. In most of the world the average annual per capita income is somewhat less than the weekly earnings of an American, Swedish, or West German factory worker. The need is imperative to raise the standards of living in the developing countries. Such change is required not to achieve luxury but simply to stay alive. What greater challenge to cross-national helping?

7. Continuing Evolution and Revolution in the Search for Power and Control in the Nations of the World

As countries develop and mature, we will see continuing change in power spectrums. New groups will develop authority, new leaders will come to the fore, and a new middle class will emerge to take its place in economic and social development. In many cases, these permutations of control and power may resemble anarchy. The U.N. General Assembly demonstrates the changing nature of this power shift. Cross-cultural consultation needs to be concerned with the issue of control and power.

8. Continuation of International Stress

This will continue to be an era of international tension. What does this mean for cross-cultural consultation? We will be counseling people who are fearful of atomic war, which will be a threat for a long time. We must help people become more aware of what to expect from themselves and others. Never has the need been so great for knowledge of behavioral sciences, economics, and religion, in order that man may better understand and cope with themselves in a physical, mental and spiritual balance.

9. Growth of Multinational Corporations and Organizations

In the 1960's and 1970's, an increasing number of multinational corporations have come into existence as the complex economic realities of the world market evolved. In addition, the number of international associations both governmental and non-governmental have multiplied. Such a growth means more inter-dependency, linkage, and collaboration across country boundaries and cultures.

These nine trends are not a complete listing of forces at work in the international scene. They are, however, a necessary minimum background for examination of cross-national consultation.

Implications of International Trends for Cross-Cultural Consultation

Let us examine these world-wide trends for implications affecting international consultants. It would seem to me that the following are clear:

1. Increased Need for Professional Management of the Social Systems in Society

More and larger institutions will develop in government, business, health and welfare, and religion. These expanding organizations will require effective managerial leadership, but the dearth of trained manpower will inhibit desirable growth, Consultation about the effective management of these organizations will be increasingly important.

2. Greater Need for Adult Education and the Use of Innovative Methods

To achieve social and industrial progress it will require much more education. The problems of illiteracy and cultural adaptation will be a challenge to the ability of educational specialists to perform their tasks responsibly. It behooves consultants to examine their educational methods and procedures to see if they are the most effective for the responsibilities that lie ahead.

3. Need for the Training of Trainers

It is quite apparent that cross-cultural consultation alone will not be able to meet the tremendous need for improved human systems. A high priority must be placed on the "training of trainers" in a particular country. Any consultation process should have as its core responsibility the multiplication process: Continuous education through transmission of expertise to other persons.

4. Need for the Process of Confrontation, Search, and Coping

The programs of cross-cultural consultation should not be seen as a means of merely communicating one person's, group's, or nation's success to that of another. It should be seen, I believe, as a *process* of helpful confrontation, search, and coping by people to solve their own problems. Persons of one culture can help those of another through dialogue. Dialogue is meaningful only if it is truly dialogue—that is, mutual. In many cases, we have tried to export our success and achievements to other countries without really attempting to reach the minds, tap the energies, and lift the hearts of people. *We* need help in how to share in a process that gives people resources to help themselves.

5. Need for Evaluation of Cross-National Consultation Services

While the process of technical assistance and cross-national consultation has been carried out for many years, there has been all too little evaluation of these programs, looking toward their improvement. Those involved in such activities should examine ways to make more effective use of their time, research, effort, and money.

6. Utilization of Multi-Disciplinary and Multiple Experience Teams

The nature of today's problems requires an inter-disciplinary approach to their solution. In too many cases, teams of specialists and consultants focus on their own specialties and do not take advantage of the variety of disciplines and experiences that could be brought to bear on the problems they confront. It seems to me that cross-national consultation teams should represent various disciplines and backgrounds for maximum effect.

7. Focusing on the Process of Change

In planning for cross-cultural consultation, we need to apply our understanding and knowledge of the processes of change, and of the learning process. In many cases, the methods we use to consult and conduct educational exchanges do not include our knowledge of how human beings learn, how they are motivated, or how they change. We are not conducting consultation just for the creation of good will or even of understanding, but to bring about a favorable change in the lives of those participating in the consultation.

8. Developing Credibility of National Consultants

There is a need for competent persons in different countries to receive recognition and to be utilized in their own country. This can be facilitated by appropriate teamwork and co-consulting with other consultants from other cultures. The maxim that "you are not a prophet" in one's own culture is too frequently the case. We need to explore ways to improve the acceptance of peers and others in our own country rather than assuming that someone from "outside" is more competent.

9. Support and Linkage Systems for Cross-Cultural Consultants

As one works in cross-cultural consultation, frequently there is a feeling of loneliness, uncertainty, and need for support. More linkages with persons similarly engaged are needed. The International Consultants Foundation has as one of its purposes helping to meet this need. More attention to sharing experiences, innovations, and professional concerns will be essential to enable cross-cultural consultations to become more competent.

Summary

This chapter is intended to set a frame of reference and to pose a challenge to those of us in consulting who wish to develop effective mobilization and utilization of human resources around the world. The challenge for those of us involved in cross-cultural exchanges is to discover those capabilities within ourselves and/or our organizations for developing meaningful consulting processes to supplement those of governments and other direct action institutions. It seems to me that the unique role of the international consultant is worthy of the eloquent challenge by the historian, Dr. Arnold Toynbee:

> ...a great world society must live not only by mind and body but by conscience and spirit as well. Is the affluence of the West simply to grow while the pressures on the poor nations steadily increase? Surely there would not be much left of its claim to humane and Christian standards if, then, it does no more than watch from the patios and bars and beaches of its prosperity, the darkness of frustration and despair spread over other lands. Indifference has never yet been the recipe for greatness or even survival. It will not prove so for the forty years that lie ahead. (1)

The international consultant's professional competence is one of responsibility, not indifference. It must, however, be developed intelligently, thoughtfully revised, and creatively undertaken. The many changes that are required in the developing countries in education, in agriculture, and in industry will have much more than economic consequences. Investment in people, new techniques, new forms of activity—all of these will widen and

---

(1) Arnold Toynbee, "Conditions of Survival," *Saturday Review,* August 29, 1964, p. 192.

strengthen the managerial and professional classes in these countries. Development of a middle class in these struggling countries will bring a brighter hope for rational politics and the equality of people.

The challenge for cross-cultural consultation is clear. The question that the ICF-sponsored "Helping Across Cultures" Conference addressed was whether we can stimulate, through professional concern, an awareness and utilization of the unique requirements of each culture so as to make cross-cultural consultation relevant and responsive to world problems both now and in the future. It is a challenge we dare not take lightly.

CHAPTER TWO
Key Issues in Cross-Cultural Consultation
by Larry Tilley and David S. Hoopes

The discussion which took place at the I.C.F. conference was wide ranging. In the process the participants identified a large number of issues which they felt the wise consultant should be cognizant of when working cross-culturally. In this chapter we have attempted to isolate out the most critical of these issues and provide some guidelines for coming effectively to grips with them. We have been relatively prescriptive in our treatment, though we recognize there is no "right way" to deal with cross-cultural issues. Circumstances vary tremendously and in some situations the very opposite of what we suggest may be the better approach. The essential ingredient of cross-cultural experience is ambiguity. In the end, it is our belief that effective cross-cultural consultation will depend most on the possession of two qualities by the consultant: (1) a respect for differences in perspective, and (2) an openness and genuiness of attitude.

In our treatment in this chapter the authors have delineated the key *cultural issues, consultant issues* and *client issues* that were identified by consulting professionals and practitioners.

Cultural Issues

1. Client resentment toward consultants who don't speak the language.

While language is significant, there may be factors which mitigate the deficiencies of not knowing the language: the ability to relate effectively; an approach that is honest, sincere and caring; and appropriate responses to a real and strong need for assistance. It may be that the need for language competence varies according to the length of the consultation. In the end, there may even be a value in not knowing the language if it reduces the threat client's may feel toward linguistically competent consultants.

2. Encountering a passive, non-participating learning style.

It may be difficult to get people to create their own structure for learning because of culture-based attitudes toward the learning experience. They may resist involvement in and ownership of the program and take less responsibility for their own learning than is desired. This can also affect the ability to get feedback during the program and to assess program quality.

3. Adapting your theoretical and/or practical model to specific client situations.

Because of cultural or situational specifics, your model, at least as presented, may be dysfunctional when implemented by the client. Your values, which are likely to be imbedded in both the theory and practice, may

be in conflict with those of the client. You will want to develop the skill to
analyze from all perspectives the chances of success or failure if your model
is implemented, and to do so with the client. It will also probably be necessary for it to be flexible enough to offer alternatives for implementation.

4. Need to discuss and negotiate role expectations.

The learning of problem solving situations must be clearly described
and the roles of those involved defined. The assignment of roles should
probably be voluntary, since there may be culture-based resistance to
playing certain kinds of roles, and care should be taken to see that both
client and consultant needs are met.

5. Creating the atmosphere of an "island of cross-cultural inquiry".

It will be of great value if an attitude of neutrality and of objective
inquiry can be fostered in the consultation. This will call for the suspension
of judgement until the issues have been explored together. It is best
accompanied by a straightforward discussion of the biases the consultant
and clients bring to the endeavor and which might inhibit the training/learn-
ing process.

6. Collecting valid data from other cultures.

When collecting data, it is best to team up with an internal consultant or
a skilled member of the host culture. Your data-gathering must take into
account cultural attitudes and behaviors and be manageable by your client.
Training of the internal consultant may be necessary to meeting this goal.

7. Establishing a new sub-culture.

In creating sub-culture, or what has been called "new culture groups,"
you will need to take much into account. In particular you will need to know
what information must be shared, what agreements need to be made, and
what norms will be expected in the new group.

**8. Helping across cultures involves the attempt to launch new sub-
cultures.**

In creating new sub-cultures you must make clear that "helping" is
defined as mutual learning and discovery and that, by design, new relationships will emerge. Clients will probably need help in coming to expect that
outcome. It will have to be discussed openly.

9. Identifying discrete cultural elements in large systems.

Data on the cultural particulars of the client's culture is extremely
valuable. A plan to collect it is important, as is a method of analyzing it in
order to draw out its significance and make it useful.

10. The feasibility of making management culture-free.

It may or may not be possible to create a culture-free management process. There is also the question: is "culture-free" synonymous with "unbiased" or "objective"? Cultural bias can, however, be minimized. There are techniques for doing so with which the cross-cultural consultant should be familiar. Cross-cultural exchange can be helpful in counteracting cultural bias.

11. Culture is the key to understanding people and their lives.

It is important to observe what is happening around you; look for value differences and appreciate their importance. A concern for culture may be as important as a concern with client needs. An understanding of culture equips you better to empathize and to communicate with clarity and understanding.

12. Becoming aware of the degree to which client attitudes toward past, present and future may differ from yours.

Planning and organizational development have an implicit future orientation. Yet clients may culturally value the present or the status quo more than what can be accomplished in the future. Change may be a negative rather than a positive phenomenon. Since the consultant is brought in to introduce change, it cannot be avoided; effective ways should be found, however, to demonstrate the more drastic implications of the changing world to which everyone must be ready to respond. It is important to communicate in this process that your ultimate goal is an improved quality of life for all.

13. Legitimization of efforts to deal with cross-cultural differences and value conflicts.

Consultant-client relationships are the key to effective delivery of services. These relationships can be enhanced by trust, openness and interdependency. This is particularly true in cross-cultural relationships where a direct approach to value difference may serve as a model for conflict management. The understanding of value differences is essential to the adaptation of consultation content to the cultural context of the client. To do this you should explore assumptions, values, communication styles, behavior patterns and ways of thinking as a part of the consultation process.

14. The degree to which cross-cultural consultation is strengthened by a thorough understanding of self.

Any client-consultant relationship can be contaminated by an insensitive consultant. Introspection and the acceptance of feedback are signs of sensitivity and help you better understand yourself and your effectiveness. Develop a performance based competency model of consultation to keep yourself on track. Be ready to collaborate with others for your own personal and professional development.

15. Coping with the loss of technical or cultural meaning when

translating between two languages.

It is important to alert clients to the multiple meanings of language. Define clearly the terms you use, especially those you know can lose or change meaning in translation. Consider developing a glossary of terms used in the communication and consultation process.

Consultant Issues

1. Consultant protecting his expertness and maintaining dependency of client.

A posture such as this can perpetuate inequality which can result in a defensive reaction in the client, created by the superiority of the 'closed expert.' It can foster a sense of client inadequacy and justify passivity and non-participative behavior.

2. Client-consultant differences.

Lack of attention to differences may create a passive or distant relationship and magnify the fear of the unknown or the fear of a lack of acceptance and/or tolerance. Avoiding these differences may inhibit the development of a mutually supportive relationship. Acknowledging and exploring differences and their implications is a powerful technique for team building and mutual acceptance.

3. Overdependency on an internal linking agent.

Undue attention to a linking agent's concerns may result in a loss of objectivity or a biased data base. This type of a relationship can reduce your responsiveness to all other representatives of the client system. Also, the continuity of the contract could be jeopardized if the internal agent is replaced.

4. Manner of presenting self: credentials, behavior, dress, language, openness.

The manner in which the consultant presents him or herself should be facilitating, not distracting. This includes being sensitive to language and behavior which may be offensive. The consultant should be comfortable and sincere with the presentation of self and not be artificial or try to impress the client.

5. Asking for feedback.

Giving feedback may not be a norm in the client's culture. In many cases the skill of giving and receiving feedback may not exist. Therefore, the consultant may have to build the training for feedback into the contract with the client. Premature requests for feedback from untrained participants could result in evaluations and judgments adversely affecting the client/consultant relationship.

6. Isolating self.

Consultants should be willing to accept the consequences of their behavior. Self-isolation may seem less risky but may have negative results, both professionally and personally. Behavior which creates a climate of involvement gives you more visibility and leaves less room for making negative assumptions about you.

7. Maintaining effective information flow.

An awareness of the impact of your style of behavior and communication and of alternative styles available to you can be a powerful tool. Maintaining unnecessary psychological distance or a superior or 'expert' posture can drastically reduce the flow of information. If your approach is genuine and involves your client intellectually and emotionally, the information flow will have a better chance of being smooth and easy to 'hear'.

8. Failure of co-consultants to model cooperative behavior.

Allowing a co-consultant to be successful without feeling threatened can be difficult. Utilizing team-building methods with your co-consultant can increase your comfort level together. Having confidence in what you do as an individual can reduce competition. Supporting the value of cooperative behavior by modeling is a powerful, positive influence on the client.

9. Clarifying who really is your client.

The person serving as internal linkage is not necessarily your client. It is essential that the consultant clearly understand the difference between the sponsor and the client. Within the client system there may be a variety of clients. The success of your project may depend upon how clear you are about who your client is.

10. The risk of taking action.

The implementation of an action plan may not produce the desired results. The fear of failure can be an immobilizing force. 'Brainstorming,' 'diagnosing' and 'action-planning' are essential skills to make one ready for the implementation stage. The ability to mobilize resources to take action can be the difference between success and failure.

11. Taking the posture of a learner.

You should be able to assume the learner's posture with your client when necessary without feeling a loss of credibility. The positive effect of your ability to take a learner's attitude can increase the quantity and quality of data made available to you. If you feel that it is important to maintain the 'expert' role, make sure you have valid data to support you.

12. Finding, involving and training appropriate inside helpers.

Inside teammates facilitate the consulting process. Compensation for the time and expense of training internal contacts can be built into the contract. This may be easier if such a decision is essential to the continuation

18

of the program after you leave. Your service would be cost-effective if you replicate yourself. Developing such internal talent can be unwieldly and may affect the future of your program in the client system.

13. Identifying common goals within the client-consultant relationship.

When the goals identified relate to data collected from all levels of the organization, you are responding to the client's goals and objectives. It is important to explore the compatibility of your goals with those of your client and identify the products anticipated. 'Doing your thing' at the client's expense is usually a result of a lack of identification of common goals and may result in a negative client-consultant relationship.

14. Legitimizing optional patterns and levels of participation among personnel.

"Once you have identified the varying needs and styles of participation, you can develop learning contracts which are tailored to needs and which are sufficiently flexible to prevent the development of guilt and hostility." This design, to be successful, requires that the participants take responsibility for their learning. The learning may be most effectively demonstrated by a competency-based design and evaluation.

Client Issues

1. Non-confrontational styles which prevent the consultant from effectively utilizing feedback.

An avoidance of confrontation reduces two-way communication and minimizes excitement in the client-consultant relationship. A lack of curiosity, interest and sharing may also result. Frequently negative situations continue instead of being corrected by feedback when non-confrontation is the norm.

2. Inability of client to articulate desire for help.

This difficulty may be related to a fear of being evaluated or judged as inadequate. It may just simply be the result of the discomfort associated with admitting that one needs help. The results of this lack of articulation may be that the consultant receives an unclear definition of needs, objectives and goals and fails to get a confirmation that help is wanted. This can result in the consultant making assumptions of need which are not real.

3. Polarization and differences within a client system.

One should avoid the development of a consultant-advocacy role and/or of a linkage with one specific subculture of the client system to the exclusion (real or perceived) of others. The consultant's values, attitudes and objectivity may be confronted here. Consultants should not avoid dealing with differences, which results in a lost opportunity for significant learning.

Understanding differences is essential to trust, openness and maximum team effectiveness.

4. Establishing a two-way learning contract.

Client objectives should be stated clearly. Consultants should be expected to state theirs too. A plan should then be developed to arrive at joint objectives.

In Summary

These three areas represent key issues that will effect a successful or unsuccessful cross-cultural consultation. Such a review is not intended to be exclusive. We hope they are realistic and helpful to improve the professional practice of consultants and the utilization of them by clients.

CHAPTER THREE
Guidelines and Principles for the Consultant in Cross-Cultural Assistance
by David S. Brown

A culture is a collection of beliefs, habits, living patterns and behaviors which are held more or less in common by people who occupy particular geographic areas. Their culture, which is the name given to this body of beliefs and practices, provides answers to the questions posed by everyday life: what to eat and not to eat, how to dress, how to greet one's neighbor or to receive one's enemy, how to work and how to play—what in short to do as one faces the problems of living. Cultures help to explain the universe: they establish its origins, settle the way it is governed, relate man to his god, and explain the diverse and often frightening actions of nature. A culture is, in short, a guide to life which is accepted by most if not all of the members of the community.

Cultures develop, we now know, over many years. They represent the experience of generations. Man's learnings over centuries are remembered, catechised, and passed along to each new generation. They are enforced in many ways.

Cultures can and do change, as men learn more about themselves and their environment. Often, however, these changes lag behind the needs of the society—which is one of the reasons why cross-cultural assistance can often be extremely helpful. Those from one culture with experience already in the requirements of the new society make available their assistance to others with need of it.

This is simple enough in theory, but as the ICF conference made clear, it is far from simple in practice. Members of the recipient culture, while eager to have many of the goods which a donor society is able to produce, are not always enthusiastic about accepting its ideas. Often they try to hold on to old beliefs and practices even though many no longer serve their original purposes.

The discussions of the conference brought out a number of major "problem areas" which the consultant/change agent will face in cross-cultural assistance. Among them:

1. Who, specifically, is the client?
2. What are the client's basic values?
3. What are the terms under which the client is willing to accept the cross-cultural change agent?
4. Who is the change agent? What are his or her motives? Values? Why is he or she there?
5. What are the primary competencies the change agent must have?

22

6. How can the consultant assure himself he is really communicating with the client ?

7. How can she help to produce a suitable learning climate?

8. What are some of the pitfalls the consultant will encounter?

1. Who, Specifically Is the Client?

The first problem the change agent encounters is that of identifying the client. On its surface this seems simple enough, but it is far from that. All groups in the final analysis consist of individuals. The change agent may be there because the group as a whole or some important sub-group within it was responsible for inviting him/her. But this does not mean that he/she will be accepted by the entire group, or even, once differences reveal themselves, by more than a minority.

The problem may be complicated still further by the fact that the cross-cultural helper may even be there because some third party—the government, a business, a church, or some other group with trans-national interests—has sent him. Perhaps only a handful of those who live in the area know who he is and why he was invited. His primary support may, indeed, come from outside sources whose concern is their own acceptance, proper though it may be, in the community.

It is one thing to say that the cross-cultural agent is there to help everyone, but it is quite another to be acceptable to all. This poses a major problem. Some in the new environment will give ready support to the new ideas. Others will feel that the consultant does not understand their problems, that he/she is basically unsympathetic to them, and that his/her very presence is destructive of existing beliefs and practices. They are quite likely to be right.

It is important, therefore, for the change agent to try to understand who their clients really are before beginning to plan what should be done and what the consultant's role in it will be.

2. What Are the Client's Values?

A culture, as we have previously noted, involves many beliefs and practices. It is a giant mosiac, made up of many individual contributions. It can be generalized, but the generalizations made of it must take into account many differences. This is why one must think also in terms of sub-cultures as well as community, family and individual patterns.

How one lives, the houses one lives in, and the complex of familial relationships all reveal the value structure. Who does what within both the family and the larger community are all a part of it. One learns the culture by observing individual dress, the foods that are eaten, the ways of preparing and serving them and, of course, the honorifics of the community. Most people are proud of their culture and quite willing to talk about it if they are approached sensitively. The change agent should not only observe, but also seek to understand why things are as they are.

Language is an important part of the culture. The meaning of particular words often holds a key to their origins. One should learn also the importance of gestures and expressions, of inflection, and of non-verbal behaviors, including body language.

Religion is a source of important values. Ideas relating to God, goodness, morality, and the hereafter must be understood by the visitor if one is to appreciate the purposes of life. One needs to learn also the patterns of governing. What is proper and improper need to be understood. One needs to know how leadership is determined, and also what the relationship of particular families is one to the other.

3. The Terms of Acceptance.

It goes without saying that the change agent must learn early in her assignment the terms under which the client (or clients) are willing to accept her.

Sometimes acceptance is easier and quicker than at other times. This may be because there is a community consensus that change is needed. Or it may be because the local leadership has been won over. Change may be the condition that an outside interest (such as a new industry) has imposed. Whatever the reason, the visitor should try to determine what has happened and why. Often, as in parts of the Orient, there may be an indication of acceptance when it is merely politeness. As soon as the agent leaves, people go back to the ancient values and traditional behaviors.

More often change is simply slow to come about and takes place only because a significant part of the population accepts it as being in its best interests to do so. While many societies (though not all) will accept the gifts the visitor brings them, including technological know-how, they may be much slower to change the value structure on which the new methodologies in the final analysis depend.

The change agent may sometimes need to show early achievement to those who have sent him/her. This will sometimes cause him/her to press for action before his/her real clients are ready for it. The results can hardly be salutatory. Whatever they may appear to be willing to do under pressure, people and values change slowly. A few warm days do not make a spring, and one should be suspicious of changes in either beliefs or behavior that come too quickly.

4. Who is the Change Agent? Why is He/She There?

No advice can be more important than the old admonition to "Know thyself". The consultant, particularly if he is from another culture, should have no misunderstanding as to why he/she is there.

If he is there because his own government has sent him (even though encouraged to do so by the host government), he should admit it to himself—and probably to others as well. One can honestly serve more than one governing agency at the same time as long as their objectives are parallel, as is often the case. One can serve a specific church without doing violence to another person's religion. One can be in another country because that country has need for physical assistance, for medical aid, for educational support, and for many other reasons which serve both the donor and donee. One can, in fact, be there because one is following one's profession which is to give advice and assistance. No one need feel embarrassed because one has personal needs to fulfill. These include the drawing of salaries that are often high by local standards.

At the same time, one must be mindful of some of the pitfalls which exist (More will be said about these later). The client will probably not see the change agent/consultant as he sees himself. Sinister motives will sometimes be read into his presence (although probably not as often as some think). Words will sometimes be misunderstood. He will be criticized for his values. There will be those who will try to frustrate his efforts, to defend the *status quo*.

The visitor should understand all of this. One should not undertake assignments such as these without a strong belief not only in the propriety of what one is trying to do but also in the equal propriety of those in the client culture who will disagree with him. After all, they seek to protect and sustain those elements of their own culture which they feel are important to them. In the final analysis the consultant should remind himself that it is the clients who must decide whether to change their ways of doing things or to continue with the old ones. The change agent who cannot accept the decisions of others, wrong-headed though he may feel they are, should not have ventured into other societies.

All of this, as was repeatedly emphasized at the conference by those with experience in other cultures, calls for a great deal of self-awareness on the part of the visitor. One must be aware of one's response to the new environment. Is there an understanding of why it is as it is? How and why has it survived as a culture? Are its strengths appreciated? There is a need here to internalize one's experiences and also to seek out new ones.

A knowledge of one's own growth processes can help in helping others to achieve growth and development. It can lead also to a kind of mutual tolerance of a variety of viewpoints.

5. The Primary Competencies the Consultant Must Have.

The conference debated at length the primary competencies the successful change agent should have.

There was agreement that the successful consultant must have a deep-seated interest in her assignment. She must want to be helpful to others and be willing to do the kinds of things that will make possible their learning.

She should take an interest not only in what people do—and how and why they do it—but should also have an interest in their history and development. It is useful that a certain amount of this be provided before the consultant's arrival, but there should be a continuing interest expressed in a concern for the social and cultural setting: the art, architecture, music, customs, etc.

The consultant's temperament should be suitable to what may frequently be an ambiguous and frustrating assignment. It may help to remember that one also gets frustrated and annoyed in one's own society where the values and behaviors are more comprehensible. This may not make the frustrations any less, but it may make them more bearable.

The consultant must also cultivate an ability to live in climate where the signals she gets from others are less likely to be understandable than they are at home, where many of them are ambiguous to begin with, and where influence is more difficult to measure. A measure of a person's maturity is her ability to continue towards agreed-upon objectives under circumstances such as these.

The consultant should have sufficient training in interpersonal skills to be able to work with a large variety of people of varying levels of conpetence. In particular, she should have had sufficient experience with "underprivileged-ness" and powerlessness to be able to exist in situations where she has only her own resources to sustain her. She should develop an ability to suspend judgment of what may be happening until she has learned more fully about it.

The consultant must be able to understand (and accept) many of the local values. (She will, incidentally, find many of them better suited to life there than her own.) In doing so, she should be aware of her own values and their importance.

She will require a social and emotional maturity strong enough to meet not only her own needs but also the needs of others, including her family, should they be with her.

Among the more useful competencies in most (but not all) circumstances is knowledge of language. The advice that most change agents will be given is to learn the language. This is basically good advice. But there are circumstances in which (1) it may not be feasible to learn the language or (2) it may be that the consultant services can be better performed by the consultant while standing apart from those he is seeking to help. This was brought home by a consultant assigned to a native Indian tribal community. He felt that his not knowing the local tongue enabled his clients to feel more free to discuss their points of view among themselves in his presence without concern that the "outsider" was overhearing them. It gave the client strength and control of the situation.

6. Is the Change Agent Really Communicating with the Client?

Feedback takes on different patterns and forms in each culture, but the need for feedback is as important in one as it is in another. The consultant/change agent must find ways of determining whether he is really communicating with those he is trying to serve.

Most of the usual methods of obtaining this feedback are likely to be pertinent. The consultant must sharpen his own listening and observing skills. Different cultures use different ways of conveying information to others. The visitor must seek methods of determining whether trust has developed, whether the client is communicating openly with him, or perhaps whether the consultant is the victim of politeness. ("Why is it," someone observed, "they always say 'yes'to whatever I ask?")

It is here that a third party, perhaps someone in the local community, can be of help. If this person shares the interests and goals of the consultant, so much the better. He or she can be greatly useful in helping the consultant to go beyond the face manifestations of interest which politeness may dictate and get at hidden feelings and judgments.

It is important that there be communication between all parties. The person from the outside must discover ways by which it can be encouraged.

7. How Can the Change Agent Help Produce a Suitable Learning Style?

Learning among adults is most productive where there is a "participant" learning style. Adults must "do" as well as "listen."

One should not be disturbed by what one member of the Bermuda group called a "raggedy start-up". It is, in fact, sometimes useful to have things begin in this fashion. The client is thus persuaded that someone is not about to impose a ready-made system upon him.

The physical setting should provide for a suitable group orientation. Groupings ought to a considerable degree to be optional. There may be both structured and unstructured exercises.

An effort should be made from the beginning to capture inputs, both from the consultant and from members of the group, by introducing the group to such learning devices as the sheet of newsprint and the colored markers which help to illustrate and record what is happening. These also provide a source of data from which future plans can be developed.

Patterns of participation should be developed as early as possible. Set speeches, by welcoming officials for instance, should not be permitted to detract from the real purposes of the group sessions. It is easier for members to introduce themselves (perhaps through some form of exercise) than to be introduced by outsiders. Socialization should be encouraged.

Although people learn differently in different cultures, there are marked similarities according to age level all over the world. Much can be adapted from one's own culture.

8. What Are Some of the Pitfalls the Consultant Will Encounter?

Each culture will have its own pitfalls, but an awareness of these will make it easier for the visiting consultant to avoid some of them.

The consultant should be aware, if she is not already so, that there will be some in the group she works with who resent the presence of an outsider. Many recipients of assistance feel that the problems they face come from beyond their borders in the first place, and they are reluctant to give outsiders greater opportunity to have influence in their society than they now have. The consultant will need to become aware of this and by doing so may be able to alleviate the resulting difficulties.

The consultant shoud avoid "experiencing for experience's sake". What is done should have basic purpose to it. It must build towards some useful goal.

Self-awareness is an important element in the learning process, but too much self-awareness can become self-centeredness. There must be a proper balance.

The approach the consultant uses may work in the majority of instances, but he must be prepared to understand that it is not necessarily best for everyone.

Major concepts are sometimes difficult to swallow whole. The change agent should devise ways by which they can be communicated, if necessary, in parts.

He should be ready to acknowledge his own mistakes.

He should not vie for a leadership role. The community is right in wanting to select its own leaders. He may be able to influence some of them later, but he must avoid seeking coalitions with them.

He should be alert to the way people see visitors who try to "go native". Host nationals often feel that the person who "goes native" is pandering to them—even though it may be genuine. The visitor can properly observe the values of his own culture. Indeed, he will probably be expected to do so.

He should avoid the "missionary complex". Rarely will it be acceptable.

Consultants should give thought to what they and their families do when they are not consulting. Consulting need not be a total-time job, nor should it be. They will be respected in their effort to enjoy the city or country. Indeed, assistance in that task will be easy to find.

In Summary

Planning what one should do as a consultant/change agent in another country or a different region of one's own country should include the taking into account of questions of the kind raised by the ICF's Bermuda Conference.

A number of these are suggested above. Because the group which discussed them was a large one, and because some of the smaller groups elected to pursue specific areas of interest, it is not possible here to do more than provide an overview of some of the main themes of discussion.

These should be discussed and evaluated by the consultant and others with knowledge pertinent to their assignments. Much that is useful will come of it. The literature of cross-cultural assistance is constantly being enlarged by the experience of practitioners. This is why the sharing of judgments concerning it is so important.

Addendum

Because one of the work groups spent considerable time in developing ways by which guidelines might be developed for cross-cultural consultants, a part of their work is appended as an addition to this chapter. It is as follows:

Selected Guidelines for Cross-Cultural Consultants

1. The consultant should be aware of values which are inherent in the client culture, and thus avoid condescending behaviors.

2. The consultant should become familiar with the significant, unique characteristics of the culture (history, geographical facts, art, contributions to other cultures, customs, religion, holidays, treatment and expectations of visitors, etc.).

3. The consultant should take considerable interest in what people in the culture do.

4. The consultant should be able to greet people in their language, and know and express several key words and phrases.

5. The consultant should ask the client to indicate cultural and technical pitfalls, expectation, potential problems, etc., prior to the visit.

6. The consultant should provide time ahead of the work engagement for relating to the culture.

7. The consultant should ask clear, open questions as opposed to closed, boxing-in questions, or over-telling, directing, giving advice, and "experting".

8. The consultant should avoid comparing the client "local" situation with another situation.

9. While applying (foreign) consultant expertise, the consultant should continuously ask the client for assistance in doing so.

10. The consultant should genuinely look for things to learn from the culture that will be of value in the consultant's own culture. (He should not be reluctant to borrow things from it; there should be a cultural exchange.)

11. The consultant should develop the attitude that the client system is not "problem people" but rather "people with a problem".

12. The consultant should develop and liberally use non-verbal models to express ideas and understandings.

CHAPTER FOUR
Methods and Techniques:
A Selected Sample of Applications For Cross-Cultural Consultation
by Leonard Nadler

There are many ways to function as a consultant in a cross-cultural situation so it is surprising that the literature is quite sparse in this area. One reason for this may be that some practitioners do not wish to "give away" their secrets or to share too openly those things which have made them successful. Fortunately, the climate within ICF and at this particular conference was one of sharing and of learning from one another. The incidents and exercises contained in this chapter were freely shared and are included here in the spirit of continuing the sharing and learning from each other.

The term "cross-cultural" is frequently misunderstood. For some, it is interchangeable with "international." As will be seen a consultant can be functioning cross-culturally within his (or her) own borders. When one leaves his own country (the geographical place) there is an expectation of a cross-cultural experience. It is important to remember that borders are arbitrary and should not determine for us where the cross-cultural experience begins.

A major area of discussion, when involving methods and techniques, is whether to adapt or adopt. There are few strategies (i.e., methods, techniques, devices) which can merely be exported. Adaptation is always necessary. The slightest adaptation can significantly change the use and meaning of a strategy.

The consultant working with another culture must always seek those strategies which are currently relevant—to the client. The consultant often seeks to use those strategies which have brought success in the past, and this is not only usual, but expected. Even when working in one's own culture, but with different clients, the experienced consultant knows that adaptations are necessary. When consulting in cross-cultural situations, it is imperative.

The methods and techniques reported in this chapter were first solicited as part of the pre-conference work of the participants. For a variety of reasons, not all participants participated in this particular exercise, though during the conference they did share much with the rest of us. This chapter is limited to those papers which were prepared before the conference, with some minor editing after the conference. I take full responsibility for any distortions, as the initial papers, in some cases, have been expanded by my recollection of what transpired during the conference. For the most part, I have tried to retain the words and certainly the feeling expressed by the contributors. They all have different styles and this is important in consulting generally and in cross-cultural consulting particularly.

To avoid confusion, let me indicate how the balance of this chapter is organized. Each contribution will start with the title presented by the contributor, and the name of the contributor(s). This will be followed by my introductory comments, in parentheses. The remainder of the section will usually be in the exact words of the contributor unless I have indicated otherwise. All of the contributions will be followed by my conclusion.

I. The Animated Film Technique

G.H. Malin

(The use of media is prevalent world-wide. Even in many lesser developed countries, it is possible to find movie projectors and other audio-visual materials. The encroachment of television into many parts of the globe has increased visual awareness among people who may have skipped the audio stage of the radio.

Malin shares with us the use of a film technique, in Canada, where the cross-cultural experience is that of city dwellers and "whites" working with rural native Indian populations.)

Malin:

"I have never lived with these people before. Their ways are strange. Help me learn something about them so when I visit their homes I don't insult them or make a fool of myself."

This statement typifies the inquiries I so often respond to. The challenge is finding ways for the community to teach the interloper (the external consultant). The animated film technique proved useful.

We solicit the cooperation of the local community school. Using 35mm film (which produces a film strip) and appropriate coaching, we have the 8-12 year old students illustrate "life in my home" by a series of drawings. When completed, we have each student provide the commentary as his film strip is projected.

By listening carefully, the external consultant will have an insightful exposure to community life, its values and beliefs and how they are manifested.

Through this, a learning-sharing process between peoples of different cultures has been initiated. Newcomers get a quick introduction to local life styles and practices. The local community learns quickly that they have something they can teach others. This technique is useful when the newcomers are persons who must visit homes and/or relate to individuals on a personal basis, such as teachers, nurses, and community workers.

This technique was originally used by us in the mid-1960's in isolated communities inhabited either by Canadian Indians or Inuits. It has been used since then with various adaptations.

Effectiveness depends on a number of conditions:

1. A relative absence of local cultural hostility toward the culture represented by the "interloper(s)."
2. The "interloper" having some cultural sensitivity and being prepared to show genuine interest.
3. Students have to be well briefed on the purpose and then allowed the freedom to do their own thing.
4. Student productions must be projected to provide sense of accomplishment and inter-student dialogue.
5. Students must be allowed to keep their own production. It is essential that the community elders know what has been said to the interlopers.

II. Use of Non-Verbal Films as Stimulus for Learning
Phyllis Lippitt and Gordon Lippitt

(The previous example dealt with a visual media which was produced within the community, understandably non-professional, to give the external person the opportunity of getting to know the community and the client.

It is possible to do something similar to this by using professionally made films, but without soundtracks! This last is crucial. Too often we see the image on the screen but have heavy dependency on the words to tell us what we have seen. The Lippitts share with us a series of films in which the absence of the soundtrack encourages the viewers to provide their own interpretations. From country to country, the consultant can expect that what the viewers see will provide valuable insight into the cross-cultural factors which must be considered.

There are times when a film with a soundtrack is important. The mistake most frequently made is to merely translate the English (or the language of the film producer) into another language as if that would bridge the cross-cultural gap. What has been overlooked is that language is a manifestation of culture. Without knowing the culture, many of the words may be meaningless and even not subject to direct translation.

The non-verbal film is an exciting technique for bridging the cross-cultural gap.

It may be considered commercial by some readers, but I am including a listing of where the films described are available. I think it would be unfair to describe them, and their usefulness, and then make the reader engage in a search for the source. Therefore, the availability is indicated with one caution. By no means are these the only non-verbal films, but they are ones used by the contributors.)

Sources of films:

Development Publications
5605 Lamar Road
Washington, D.C. 20016
Tel.: (301) 320-4409

(Sells and distributes
all the films mentioned)

Stephen Bosustow Productions
P.O. Box 2127
Santa Monica, CA 90406
Tel.: (213) 394-0218

(Produced films #2, #3, #5,
#6, and #7)

Phoenix Films, Inc.
470 Park Avenue
New York, NY 10016

(Produced and distributes
film #1)

Lippitt and Lippitt:

In a number of countries we have found the use of well made but short films (usually with cartoons) that do not have a particular spoken language on the sound strip can be a very valuable learning experience. These films, made in different countries do not have to be "dubbed" with the language of that country or culture. The consultant/trainer can develop the group diagnostic questions for watching and discussing in their own language prior to the showing of the film. The film is not "cultural biased" by a particular language. It has the advantage of visualization in learning. It also puts a serious problem in perspective. It develops an opportunity for creative thinking and alternative expression. We have used these films in Australia, Brazil, Denmark, England, Finland, Holland, Japan, Mexico, Puerto Rico, and Venezuela.

We have found the following films to be effective in cross-cultural settings:

1. **REFINERS FIRE**
   Length: 10 minutes (16mm, color)
   A gripping abstract presentation of the difficulties of initiating change, utilizing animation and music. Unique and effective in promoting discussion.
   Training use: Understanding change; causes of resistance to change; strategies in initiating change.

2. **GOOD GOODIES**
   Length: 4½ minutes (color)
   A whimsical film that raises questions about the problems created by over-advertising without identification and articulation of customer needs.
   Training use: Needs census; influencing others.

3. A BETTER TRAIN OF THOUGHT
Length: 10 minutes (16mm, color)
A film designed as an introduction to any training program in which management development is the method or theme. A delightfully animated look at the fact that as we approach problems we tend to rehash and rearrange elements we're most familiar with while finding it harder to employ new elements or solutions.
Training Use: Creativity; problem solving; group action.

4. DIVIDED MAN
Length: 4½ minutes (16mm, color)
The increasingly complex dilemmas of coping with a world where choices multiply daily is presented in a simple, graphic manner in this unusual short film. A solitary figure travels down a road until confronted with a fork and must decide which way to go. The figure hesitates; there is no indication of what lies ahead on either path. Instead of making the choice, the figure divides itself in two in an attempt to travel both parts. The two paths join back into one road again and the two-halved person attempts to reunite—with surprising results. The significance of commitment and choice are just some of the questions raised in this provocative film.
Training Use: Decision making; leadership; supervisory training; organizational development.

5. JOSHUA AND THE BLOB
Length: 7 minutes (16mm, color)
Joshua's experience with the blob helps us to consider the effectiveness of an open and positive attitude in responding to new ideas, to unknowns, and unusual situations.
When approached by the blob, Joshua responds with fear and hostility. As he grows to know the blob, his relationship with it becomes a happy one. This experience relates to any we may have with organizational changes. The most positive attitude is the most productive one.
Training Use: A film for human relations, team-building, communications.

6. JOSHUA IN A BOX
Length: 5 minutes (16mm, color)
Joshua is confined to a box. The unique predicament, his attempts to escape and the emotional response to frustration can be interpreted on many levels and in various ways. To promote creative and critical thinking, the film poses these fundamental questions:

- How does a person react to freedom?
- How does a person cope with confinement or restriction?
- Is it the individual's fate to remain imprisoned by emotional needs and responses?

Training Use: Creativity; problem solving, self-help programs.

7. JOSHUA AND THE SHADOW

Length: 9½ minutes (16mm, color)

This Joshua film teaches us that we must be in control of our inner emotional forces and that we must recognize the anxieties that often seem to be "out there" are really internal.

Joshua reacts to the discovery of his own shadow with responses ranging from avoidance to aggression. He discovers a tool, a light, with which we can control his shadow...that light is symbolic of a tool with which we can control our emotional shadows...understanding.

Training Use: Self imaging; personal growth; self in relation to organizations.

For the films to be used effectively, the following should be considered:

1. Good physical facilities and projectors. The films are short and some viewers may have difficulty, for they are waiting for the verbal portion.
2. Before the showing - a set of questions in the language of the country to give a "mind set." Particularly, emphasis on the non-verbal aspect.
3. Make observation assignments for later discussion.
4. Use of small groups to discuss the film with resource person and then relating the group's learning to concepts, theory, and practice.

III. Perceptual Exercise

David S. Hoopes

(It would be unlikely to find many consultants who do not have a series of exercises they have found helpful. There are many learning strategies, and exercises are one of the most useful. They provide the participant with a direct experience which the consultant can then build upon to elicit the personal feelings and perceptions of the learner.

Recognizing that the many exercises rely on verbalization, there has been an increased tendency to use non-verbal exercise, even among people from the same cultures. The non-verbal becomes even more helpful when used with people from different cultures.

When using an exercise, it is important for the consultant (or learning facilitator) to provide for a synthesis. Without this, there is no way to determine whether learning has taken place, and if so, what kind.

The following description is based on notes provided by Hoopes and supplemented by my observation as he demonstrated the exercise to us.)

Hoopes:

I use exercises to demonstrate perceptual differences among people of different cultural backgrounds. A number of exercises are used to bring home to those participating, the degree to which they perceive even simple basic symbols differently - how they respond differently and read into them their own meanings and emotions.

This particular exercise can be used with a group of anywhere from 10 to 50 people. Ideally, the group would be multi-cultural but that is not necessary. It can be used anywhere a chalkboard or flip chart is available. It takes from 20 minutes to a half hour. It can be used in the context of a larger program or activity, or it can be the basic focus of the experience. It can be a base on which to build further training or consulting activities.

The exercise calls for the facilitor to draw a symbol on the board and to have each individual write down the first word that comes to mind upon seeing the symbol. Then, go around the room and have each person call out the word they wrote in response to the symbol. This is then repeated with the next symbol, and so on. Each time, it will be readily apparent that the same symbol evokes different responses. The symbols which can be used are a plus sign, a six pointed star, a wavy line, a swastika (or the Buddhist symbol which is different), etc. The symbols should be uncomplicated.

Several things are accomplished by this demonstration. The participants have an enjoyable and involving personal experience. Perceptual theory is brought to the personal level out of the clouds of psychology. A participatory ethos or atmosphere of involvement is created which has carryover to other parts of the program.

This demonstration can be useful in almost any circumstance, since it is so rare that we are confronted with and can experience the degree to which our perceptions are personally unique and culturally conditioned.

While this is not part of the helping process itself, it seems that achieving a common experience with and understanding of perceptual differences across cultures is a sine-qua-non of cross-cultural helping.

IV. Using Cross-Religion for Cross-Cultural Learning
Peggy Lippitt

(There is little doubt that religions are culturally based. Even the same religion, when practiced in a different culture, will develop different rituals and customs. As with many other cross-cultural experiences, one learns as much about one's self as about the other culture. In this example, P. Lippitt shows how religion can be used to expand an appreciation and understanding which might not be possible when a person focuses only on their own religion.)

Lippitt:

The better understanding of one of the most important Buddhist concepts, that of liberation: i.e., freedom from the bondage of one's own preconditioned ways of responding to life situations. While such a goal cannot be achieved in one series of group meetings, there are concepts and skills that can be learned which help one realize growth in that direction. It is a new way to look at personality development and to effect freedom from attitudes and habits that no longer serve a useful purpose.

This was used in application of Eastern (Buddhist) concepts to groups in family living and child rearing. These groups were designed for parents and teachers with a primarily Western philosophy and orientation—hence the cross-cultural component of this innovation. It was used (1) in a group studying "Application of Buddhist Concepts to Parent Education and Family Living" offered by the Nyingma Institute of Colorado, Boulder, Colorado, in the 1977 winter term; (2) in an in-service course offered parents and teachers of the Montessori schools in Ann Arbor, Michigan, during the fall of 1977.

The first group session included a conceptual input about "self-image" as the result of the dualistic mind which sees things and itself as "separate", as subject-object. This (these) self-image(s) or picture(s) of oneself as separate generate feelings and thoughts which motivate specific actions. One's personality is the sum total of these self-images which one has collected and which continue to effect one's actions. Participants are given an exercise which helps them retrieve a self-image of their own and identify the thoughts, feelings and actions it generates. Later they are introduced to the possibility of dissolving a self-image, thereby becoming liberated from the conditioned responses it activates.

This is a way to help those brought up with a Western philosophical orientation to understand that, (1) the ego, which to the Buddhist is that which thinks of itself as separate, is *not* a reality. It is a thought construct of our mind (and very real to us); (2) that non-ego does not mean the loss of *life*, the loss of *being*, for we are life, we are being. What it does mean is liberation from the prisons we have built for ourselves—loneliness—separativeness—no goodness.

To be effective, there should be an interest on the part of participants to explore something new. Also care to connect this innovative conceptual material with theories and practices already accepted and proved useful in the Western culture—thereby showing that Western and Eastern concepts and techniques, although different, are not necessarily incompatible.

V. Using a Written Memorandum

Leonard Nadler and Zeace Nadler

(Using a written memorandum may not seem new, innovative, or even unusual. We do it all the time, but usually not in a consulting relationship. The written memorandum carries with it the same possibility of cultural misunderstanding that can be found in other verbal approaches. The purpose was not to reduce everything to writing, but rather to use the memorandum as a device for further clarification.

This technique must be approached with caution. In too many cultures, the written word becomes a fact. Once it is written, changing it becomes a major activity if not an impossibility. In such cultures, the written word should not be taken lightly. To produce a written document overnight, as described in the example, would be either impossible or impolite. When the written word is that important, it is expected that one take sufficient time to produce the appropriate words.)

Nadler and Nadler:

After each day of the consulting relationship, the consultants prepared a memorandum which was a summary of what had been discussed and accomplished that day.

Reducing something to writing may not appear innovative. In cross-cultural consulting we tend to think that language may get in the way of understanding, and therefore place a high reliance on direct communication, hoping that this will minimize the language confusion.

Our own experience, in non-confronting countries, has been that people need time to react to what has happened. They need to be able to avoid the confrontation of being asked directly if agreement has been reached. The written memorandum provides the mechanism for narrowing down areas of disagreement or confusion without causing that direct confrontation.

We first used this in Thailand. We were helping a group develop a budget to seek funds for a program. They presented us with a budget which was completely unrealistic, so we began moving them towards a modified MBO approach for which a budget could be produced. They had never done this before and wanted to rely on numbers, no matter how meaningless.

At the end of the first morning, we left, and they agreed to consider talking of objectives rather than budget. When we returned to our hotel and reviewed the morning, we found that we had some differing perceptions of how the Thais were reacting. We decided to try to clear up the situation by producing a brief written memo of what had taken place, with particular emphasis on why we were suggesting the objective approach. We prepared a typed memo, only about three quarters of a page, with copies for each member of the group.

The next morning, before the meeting, we met with the senior person and suggested that we were not clear on what had happened the day before (a typical statement in a non-confronting society) and would appreciate it if they would help us by reading the memo and letting us know if that was what they heard us recommend, and if we had reflected what they had been telling us. After reading the memo, he agreed.

The meeting started with this memo, and the group then voiced their opinion in terms of their reactions to the memo rather than as personal statement. This allowed for much more input than would usually have been acceptable in a non-confronting society.

The rest of the week we proceeded in the same manner. We prepared a memo each day, and each day, asked for their help. The experience was extremely successful and resulted in the client making a complete change and fully accepting the objectives approach as a way of proceeding.

We used the same approach in Malaysia, where we were designing a training program. Also a non-confronting society, the group appeared to be having difficulty in providing some needed information about how to determine training needs. Once again, we used the memo approach. It proved extremely useful in getting them to provide information about the politics involved in job appointments, the difficulty in asking people to "list" anything, and some of the history of "training" programs in the past. (Actually, merely presenting the job description.) The daily memos provided a focal point where the consultants were asking the client for help in understanding and the client was pleased to respond.

From our own experience, it is most useful in a non-confronting environment. Where there is a difference in language, that can be used as the reason for reducing it to writing. The memo should be kept short, usually no more than a page. It should be specific, but can raise questions that the consultants have and to which the client can respond.

The memo should not be used to force agreement, but rather to seek clarification during the consulting relationship.

VI. The Use of a Motivation Checklist in International Training/Consultation

Gordon L. Lippitt and E. Bruce Peters

(The use of instruments and checklists is well known among consultants. It is rare to find the consultant who does not have a series of these for a variety of situations. Lippitt and Peters share one of theirs with us, but also indicate some of the advantages and limitations in the use of any instrument.

Where language is a problem, an instrument can lose its entire validity when translated. Caution should be exercised in taking a well-researched instrument and exporting it to another culture. The same instrument can be used, however, if it is carefully and effectively translated. It may not be entirely appropriate, though, to compare the results as if all the respondents had received the same instrument, when some used the original, and others the translation.

The instrument described here was used for training and consultation, and not for research. Its use is carefully delineated.)

Lippitt and Peters:

Confronted with a cross-cultural training situation, the authors have used data collection instruments to gain flexibility, adaptability, and bridge the cultural and language gap. While the frame of reference here is international, many of the advantages might also apply in other training contexts. Here is how the utilization reported in this article occurred:

"Can you go to South America next month to speak on motivation and productivity?" was the request from a representative of the State Department. Brazil, Colombia, Peru and Chile were the countries to be visited.

The Bureau of Educational and Cultural Affairs wanted to try a different type of specialist in their program, someone with a management orientation. Lacking previous experience in this subject area, little was known about the size, interests, or background of the groups on the schedule. Even the designation of the groups was not learned until after arrival in the country in many cases. Defining and adapting to group interests could only be done as a part of the presentation itself.

The lack of prior information lessened the appropriateness of any kind of set presentation. The need for flexibility indicated the choice of motivation instrument and a participative method as a technique to adapt to the audience needs.

The instrument used is shown in Figure 1 and has been translated into Spanish, Portuguese, French, and Dutch. This is an instrument developed by Leslie This and Gordon Lippitt (1).

The authors used this instrument for 10 years with over 10,000 employees. Those filling out the instrument were foremen, middle managers, vice presidents, and chief executive officers. In this period of

---

(1) This instrument was used with over 10,000 employees in U.S.A. from 1962 to 1972. The authors developed the original checklist into a diagnostic training instrument entitled "Work Motivation Checklist" published by Development Publications, 5605 Lamar Road, Washington, D.C. 20016.

Figure 1

"FACTORS WHICH TEND TO MOTIVATE ME"

Please indicate the *five items* from the list below which you believe are most important in motivating you to do your *best work* for your organization.

1. _____ Steady, secure employment
2. _____ Respect for me as an individual
3. _____ Knowing I will be held responsible for my own performance
4. _____ Good pay
5. _____ Good physical working conditions
6. _____ Chance to turn out quality work
7. _____ Getting along well with others on the job
8. _____ Chance for promotion
9. _____ Opportunity to do creative and challenging work
10. _____ Pensions and other fringe benefits
11. _____ Being able to participate in the decisions that affect me
12. _____ Not having to work too hard
13. _____ Knowing what is going on in the organization
14. _____ The organization's interest and concern for social problems (i.e., ecology, pollution, service to other organizations, etc.)
15. _____ Feeling my job is important
16. _____ Having a written job description of the duties for which I am responsible
17. _____ Being commended by superior when I do a good job
18. _____ Getting a performance rating, so I know where I stand
19. _____ Attend staff meetings
20. _____ Agreement with organization's objectives
21. _____ Large amount of freedom on the job
22. _____ Opportunity for self-development and improvement
23. _____ Having an efficient and competent superior
24. _____ Knowing I will be disciplined if I do a bad job
25. _____ Working under close supervision
26. The organization's willingness to let me spend time working on community activities
27. _____ _____
    _____
28. _____ _____
    _____
29. _____ _____
    _____
30. _____ _____
    _____

utilization the seven items most frequently indicated by all persons were as follows:

Good pay	62%
Respect for me as a person	61%
Chance for promotion	59%
Knowing what is going on in the organization	51%
Opportunity for self-development and improvement	75%
Feeling my job important	73%
Opportunity to do interesting work	71%

The results may have been influenced by the fact that the administration was done during a Management Development activity. The sample included managers from industry, government, education, voluntary agencies, and trade associations.

Use in Other Countries:

The instrument was used with over 400 professional society persons in four countries. It was also used with university students and faculty, engineers, consulting groups, and top business management groups. The results in each country may be of interest to students and practitioners of cross-cultural training or managers working in other countries. Such a study will be reported in a forthcoming article by the authors.

There is no inference here that used with these multi-national groups revealed scientifically valid results concerning differences in motiviation in different countries. However, the instrument shown here did highlight apparent differences in motivation reflecting cultural, political, and economic differences. While not scientifically validated, results do reveal how the population surveyed view themselves.

Further, the results emphasize the heterogeneity one experiences during a visit to South America. We may have a tendency to think of South Americans as homogeneous despite knowledge to the contrary. These results again emphasize the differences.

Method of Checklist Utilization:

The instrument served as a springboard for a broader discussion of motivation. It was introduction to the ideas of prominent theorists in a way that was most relevant to the individuals concerned. It portrayed in graphic relief their interests and assumptions.

Among the broader uses, flexibility and adaptability were primary reasons already mentioned. An instrument can also be a great help when dealing with large groups. The large group can be sub-divided to use the instrument as a focal point for discussion. In this way, the trainer can use

44

small group techniques conducive to learning, attitude and behavioral change.

Interest was heightened and each person in the audience could be personally involved with the presenter, the subject matter, and other participants. Conversely, it also gave the resource person a sense of individual contact.

A sense of immediacy resulted from the action research aspects. Feedback of data collected was practically instantaneous thus increasing the impact of the subject matter. In this way, it helped bridge the cultural and language barriers. The resource person was not an advocate of some foreign philosophy speaking a strange tongue but an assistant helping participants interpret their own data and give it meaning.

Values in Use of Instruments:

This one example of instrument utilization reflects the authors' belief that instruments, translated for that particular culture have many advantages.

1. **Value of Involvement**
   The use of an instrument, as cited in our previous example, can increase the involvement of persons in the learning/action process.

2. **Economic Values**
   The use of an instrument can collect data quicker and more economically then the utilization of consultants' lengthy interviews or longitudinal studies.

3. **Efficiency of Administration**
   Instruments can be administered to a group in a short space of time. A lot of data can be secured with a minimum effort and time.

4. **Variety of Utilization**
   Instruments can be used to diagnose, educate, direct, and serve as source of corrective action.

5. **Provides a Degree of Objectivity**
   Utilizing instruments can provide a larger sample and therefore a degree of objectivity that a few interviews or opinions would not provide.

6. **Data Comparison**
   If one uses instruments utilized in other settings, it is possible to compare data as we have done in this example.

7. **Provides Trend Data**
   The information on an instrument can provide a trend that can be diagnostic for trainer, participant, or management.

8. **Opportunity for Immediate Feedback**
   An instrument can provide immediate feedback to an individual,

group or management as to their assumptions, feelings, or beliefs.

9. Provides Stimulus for Action

An instrument can give data for corrective action by the individual, group, or organization.

Cautions on Use of Instruments:

While these values sound like a non-critical endorsement of instruments, we should point out some weaknesses to instrument utilization.

In using the instrument there will be sociological and psychological variables in the situation. For example, if the instrument is diagnosing management styles during a human resource development program, participants may respond to Theory "Y" assumptions because of the influence of the situation.

Instrument data may not be valid or reliable in terms of the instrument used or population utilized.

It also may be misused by collecting data and then not using it for diagnosis, learning, or action.

Effectively used, however, the authors have found that instruments like the Motivation Checklist are valuable resource tools in consultation and training to provide learning, change opportunities, and action taken by participants.

VII. Culture Shock Test

William J. Reddin and Ken Powell

(This is another type of instrument. The focus is more on self-awareness in a cross-cultural context. The purpose is to lessen the effect of culture shock.

A good deal has been written about this phenomena. Despite this, there is still much more we need to know. Some people do very well in moving into another culture and experience little or no shock. They are culturally mobile and do not even need to know the language to somehow survive and even be successful. They are unique and we need to know much more about them.

For most people, cultural moves can be frightening and even completely debilitating. When people must take time to adjust, their effectiveness is lessened and the cost of their services can skyrocket. Therefore, there is a constant search for kinds of instrumentation which will help us understand more about ourselves, before we are engaged in a cross-cultural situation. The instrument described here can be used in that way.)

Reddin and Powell:

The Culture Shock inventory is designed to acquaint those who expect to work outside their own culture with some of the things that may disorient them. Culture shock is a psychological disorientation caused by misunderstanding, or not understanding, cues from another culture. It arises from such things as lack of knowlege, limited prior experience and personal rigidity. The eight scales test for Western ethnocentrism (the belief that the West's way is generally best), cross-cultural experience, cognitive flex, behavioral flex, cultural knowledge specific, cultural knowledge general, customs acceptance, interpersonal sensitivity. The following are some examples of items on the different parts of the inventory.

A. Lack of Western Ethnocentrism

The degree to which the Western value system is seen as possibly inappropriate for other parts of the world.

"A great many countries would not benefit from increased industrialization."

"In a great many ways, people in lesser developed countries have a better life than those in industrialized countries."

B. Experience

The degree of direct experience with people from other countries through working, traveling and conversing, and also learned skills such as reading and speaking foreign languages.

"People from other countries are often invited to our home."

"As an adult, I have had at least one very close friend from another country."

C. Cognitive Flex

The degree of openess to new ideas and beliefs and the degree to which these are accepted by the individual.

"I am never called opinionated."

"It is always best to be completely open-minded and willing to change one's opinions."

D. Behavioral Flex

The degree to which one's own behavior is open to change.

"I have done some very unusual things that have changed my life."

"I often experiment with new methods of doing things."

E. Cultural Knowledge - Specific

The degree of awareness and understanding of various beliefs and patterns of behavior in specific other cultures.

"America is thought to be less class conscious than Britain.

"Germans are believed to form and join clubs more than people from most other countries."

F. Cultural Knowledge - General

The degree of awareness and understanding of various beliefs and institutions in other cultures.

"No languages are inferior to other languages.

"Countries which have no system of courts can still provide adequate justice for their people."

G. Cultural Behavior - General

The degree of awareness and understanding of verbal and nonverbal human behavior.

"People in lesser developed countries do not behave in unnatural ways."

"Work and play are not clearly different."

H. Interpersonal Sensitivity

The degree of awareness and understanding of verbal and nonverbal human behavior.

"The way a person stands can tell you something about him as a person."

"A person's facial expression can change the meaning of the spoken word."

Up to this time, the most effective use of the Inventory is for training. After further use, and the collection of sufficient data, it is possible that it may be shown to have predictive power.

It's major use has been with 648 North American managers though it has been used in other situations, such as in the Peace Corps.

VIII. The Inside-Outside Consultation Team
Eva Schindler-Rainman and Ronald Lippitt

(Many people have the image of consultants being loners. Each comes in and does "their thing" and then slips away. Some clients may even feel it signifies a weakness when a team (two or more) of consultants is utilized.

There are times when a one-on-one relationship is important for a consulting relationship. There are also situations which require that the consultation be accomplished through a team effort.

Consultants frequently agree that within the client system, teams (and its corollary of team building) are essential when trying to bring about organizational change. It appears satisfactory for the client to have a team, but less appropriate to the consultant.

The example given here highlights that there are situations when consultants, functioning as a team, are the desirable way to accomplish the objectives.)

Schindler-Rainman and Lippitt:

The experience described here focuses on the development and utilization of a cross-culture, cross-language, inside-outside consultation and training team. The consultants were from the U.S., the client from Spain.

48

Through correspondence with the client (National Institute for Education, Madrid), the U.S. consultants were able to indicate the need for an internal pair of consultants. It was recommended that one of the pair be selected with more senior and academic status, and the other with more identity with the internal staff of the organization. Memos were exchanged on the proposed role in collaboration and the U.S. consultants then sent the first draft of a needs and expectations assessment instrument. The client was to process this by revision, translation, and distribution to the client population. The inside team received the responses, summarized and sent them to the outside team who used the data to develop a tentative draft of the design for the consultation-training activity. It also served as guidelines for resource materials the outside team was to send to have duplicated by the inside team.

The outside team arrived in the host country and spent the first day in planning and team building with the inside team. Together, they revised the design, reviewed the physical arrangements and modified as needed, provided political linkages, clarified the egalitarian status relations, and rehearsed their plans for cross-language communication.

During the week of consultation and training, translation was provided when needed. Small groups worked in Spanish on newsprint and the inside team summarized the material on the sheets for the outside team. Feedback group interviews were conducted by the inside team.

In retrospect, this pattern of work ensures much greater diagnostic sensitivity to the cross-cultural client system, reduces risks through joint planning, provides on-going process feedback to reduce traps of miscommunication and differences of expectations. Also ensures a mechanism for followup and continuity after outsiders leave.

The outside team has used this same approach in Nurenberg with the U.S. Army Morale Services, YMCA in Canada, and with the Japanese National YMCA.

To be effective, the inside team should be genuinely on a peer level. There must be time for an exchange of memos and data collection. There must be a mutual commitment, between the teams, to this concept of collaboration.

IX. Improving Productivity by Eliminating Marginal Work
Herman P. Hoplin

(The effective utilization of the work force is a pervasive problem. In lesser developed countries, there tends to be a proliferation of almost meaningless tasks in order to assure that there are as many jobs as can possibly be made available. The over-staffing tends to slow down operations and considerably increases labor costs.

The alternative is to have fewer jobs and large pockets of unemployed who can easily be swayed to participate in demonstrations, terror, and other forms of violence. They have little to lose.

Trapped in this apparent Hobson's Choice, there are many countries that recognize that unless they can increase productivity they cannot compete in the world and will face economic decline and political destruction.

Hoplin shares with us an experience where the decision was made to increase productivity even though one cost is the possible reduction of the work force by eliminating marginal work. Fortunately, other alternatives were possible for those displaced.)

Hoplin:

This experience concerns the elimination of unchallenging/marginal work and the "boxing off" of personnel excess to the essential work force requirements. Substantial numbers of the workers who were not only superfluous, but were actually in the way of those performing essential production jobs, were physically transferred to reclamation and renovation projects where they could accomplish useful tasks until the project was completed or they were trained and absorbed back into the plant's production operations. (On the current scene poor quality of working life remains detrimental to productivity. Excess personnel are one of the most debilitating elements in an organization. This innovation seeks to make all workers productive.)

The experience was used in an organization (process plant) of approximately 650 people in the Middle East where productivity was less than 50% of the plant capacity. The plant was not a labor intensive operation, but extra personnel had been added to the rolls to compensate for low skills in a futile effort to improve productivity.

The experience boosted morale in the plant which resulted in better housekeeping and production rates. The innovation is a "must" in a process or automated plant where unskilled management is likely to hire unskilled workers in an attempt to "beef" up production by substituting brawn for technical skill.

This experience permitted fast results and productivity increases from the low 40% level to 85% in a matter of weeks. Technical improvements would then be employed for an additional 10% productivity increase. The innovation's possibilities are great where a consultant needs to get fast results. As an added bonus, pilferage in the plant decreased drastically when employees became occupied with useful tasks and morale ascended from a low ebb toward a respectable level.

CONCLUSION

The examples presented here represent the actual experiences of practicing consultants in cross-cultural situations. Each has shared openly what they have done in particular situations so that the rest of us can benefit from their experiences. Of course, we learn from our own behavior but should be encouraged to utilize some of the resources and techniques discussed in this chapter.

The material presented here is dated. None of the contributors would want to be known only for these experiences, nor do they want to be trapped by them. Practicing consultants are constantly innovating and experimenting. New techniques, instruments, aids and devices are constantly appearing-and disappearing. It is most important that we continue to improve the methods and techniques used in cross-cultural situations, and that we continue to share them with each other.

CHAPTER FIVE
Future Images of Cross-Cultural Consultation
by Ronald Lippitt, David Hoopes and Gordon Lippitt

If this volume constitutes a kind of initial examination of the nature and requisites of cross-cultural consultation, it behooves us at the end to step back and take a look at some of the broader issues which confront us now and/or loom in the immediate future. It was decided to do this in the form of a conversation between the editors and Ronald Lippitt, a participant in the Bermuda Conference and a person whose long experience in consulting and training around the world would help us obtain the desired breadth of perspective. The discussion centered around five questions:

DAVID:

1. What are the multi-national consulting needs in today's world?

RONALD:

It seems to me that one need is the multi-national corporation where the corporation is utilizing a mix of personnel from both inside and outside the host culture. In this process there develops needs for communication training and consultation on communication about cross-cultural differences between persons who are having to work together.

GORDON:

Another area that I observe in the international field is increased nationalistic pride in one's own roots. As a consequence there tends to be more suspicion, lack of trust and confidence in a consultant from another country. We need to develop and utilize persons within their own culture or who know the other culture well. The need for cross-cultural support through consultants who know that particular nationality, culture, ethnic group, etc. is very essential.

RONALD:

You're suggesting the need for *teaming* in consultation. For example, it might be desirable that where two cultures are being consulted with, the persons that are being consulted may have some basis of distrust and conflict and it may be that a third party representative may be needed on the team.

DAVID:

Our experience is that in cross-cultural research and analysis the perspective of a single culture is almost inevitably inadequate. Two cultures are better, while three constitutes the optimum, giving you a check, as it were, on the biases of the two principals.

Another area that is very important for the multi-nationals today is their dealings with host governments. Multi-nationals are intricately entangled with host governments all over the world. The consultant, for instance, who can help them understand better the perceptions and the culture-based motivations which influence political action of host governments will provide a valuable service. The consultant is going to have to be aware too of cross-cultural relations within a country. One corporation which is operating in Malaysia, for instance, has had to be concerned not only with American relations with Malays, but with Chinese-Malay relations as well.

GORDON:

We've discussed examples of multi-national corporations. I think the same thing can be said of international organizations, including UN and UNESCO, including the World Council of Churches, YMCA, etc., where you see the phenomenon where an international organization may get smug about the fact that they have somebody from that country on their staff, but they may have been living in Geneva for 12 years, and even though they come from a South American country they may have lost contact with some of the recent developments in their own country. I think there is a need for having a team so as to update the realities of the cross-cultural situation. We can get "culture bound" even when working in another country.

RONALD:

I think also of multi-cultural consultation needs that are not just focused on organizations but are focused, for example, on the schools. When I worked on the staff of the International School in Geneva there were young people from some 15 to 20 cultures and nationalities, and teachers from five or six. The inservice training needs of that faculty were a critical need.

Or of course the needs of the families who are living in the communities with cross-cultural neighbors.

GORDON:

There's the whole matter of training the influencers whether they are teachers, administrators, or technicians in cross-cultural sensitivity.

2. What competencies should consultants have in order to meet the needs of multi-national organizations?

GORDON:

Certainly, one competency is being sensitive to one's own culture and appreciating the same, as well as being sensitive to and appreciating other cultures with which you work. Second, is the whole matter of acquiring some modicum of self insight, and developing understanding of one's self vis-a-vis one's own hangups, your own prejudices, preferences, likes and dislikes, so that we know about them. We're not talking about a perfect person, with no hangups, but understanding your own self. These are two competencies that come to mind.

RONALD:

It seems to me that one of the sensitivities or insights consultants need is to be aware that although you may be comfortable in and feel you understand the culture, it doesn't mean that as an outsider that you have credibility there. It's one thing to feel comfortable and knowledgeable about the culture and another to be able to work effectively in terms of acceptance and credibility. Therefore it seems to me the competence in *teaming* with insiders rather than assuming that because you feel comfortable you can go it alone, is an important area of competence.

GORDON:

Right. That makes me think of a fourth one, and that is the need for the cross-cultural consultant to be very skilled in linking resources. The ability to link resources between themselves and other internal resources of the country, external resources outside the country, and resources of the client they are serving in the country. The skill to see oneself as a linker of resources is even more needed in a cross-cultural consultation where you may not have the resources to tackle the complete aspects of the problem because of the complexity of the problems in cross-cultural settings.

RONALD:

It seems to me another competence is not getting trapped into assuming that certain individuals in the culture that appear to be speaking for others really are representative. The need to be aware of the kind of "sensing out" through some internal tests of people who are really key people to be worked with rather than assuming that because somebody has a good facility in your language and are knowledgeable about what's going on, that they're necessarily the people you want to depend upon for data or as sources.

GORDON:

Right. I think that's why I would list as the sixth competency the need for the cross-cultural consultant to be a diagnoser. Every consultant has to be a diagnoser, but in the cross-cultural situation, as Ronald has indicated, there is a temptation to jump at conclusions and assumptions. That's why some American consultants are having difficulty in doing business in the Mideast because we don't understand well enough their culture. A shake of the hands will not be a contract in Saudi Arabia, where it may be in Vermont. The cross-cultural consultant has to go overboard, almost, in diagnosis; they have to have the skill to look at the problem many more times, get additional data, and to thoroughly check the complexities of the situation.

DAVID:

I think one of the assumptions that cross-cultural consultants have to make is that they cannot make any assumptions. They must also have the ability to deal with ambiguity. That is important. There are two kinds of ambiguity which one will or at least may have to deal with. One is the ambiguity inherent in cross-cultural situations because you simply cannot know enough not to have the situation be ambiguous. The other lies in the fact that there are many cultures in which ambiguity is woven into the style of communication and human relations.

GORDON:

Yes, that's another competency we're implying. I would like to emphasize the skill of *role flexibility* by the consultant. To be able to manifest not only the different roles on the spectrum of directiveness to non-directiveness that Ronald and I have put in our book, but also of being able to be at one stage a father confessor, at another stage a writer, another time a teacher, and another time a mediator.

I think also one role is just to represent your own country. As a person from a particular country you can't escape that role and I don't think you should.

3. How can consultants acquire the needed competencies?

GORDON:

Well, I'd like to start off by suggesting three things, one, to broaden their own experience by working in different cultures to secure a broader perspective. Don't just work with one country besides your own, work with five or six; secondly, as much as possible develop opportunities to pair up with a colleague, even though you might have to lessen or share the fee and you might have to talk the client into accepting a team so you can give each other feedback, observe each other's performance, and grow as a result of the teaming experience; and third, I think more attention to evaluation so that during and at the end of the client relationship, time is given and procedures are used to secure evaluation. I just reviewed the other day a consulting evaluation form used by one of the large accounting firms. They have a very helpful evaluation process which they use with each of their consultants at the end of a consulting project. Many of us do not do this systematically enough, and I think those of us working in cross-cultural consultations have a responsibility to build in the evaluation so we can get feedback and develop our competencies.

RONALD:

It takes some work to get debriefing accepted as a normal thing to do, for example, when you're working with Japanese colleagues. There's a certain amount of hesitation as to whether you could really develop this kind of relationship so as to protect the pride and respect of each party.

We found in working with Japanese colleagues on an international YMCA project that it was really important to make an official project out of talking about the consulting process as a legitimate part of the learnings.

DAVID:

I think in a more simple vein, and perhaps anticipating the next couple of questions, there are groups and organizations such as ICF, SIETAR and the Intercultural Network which are in the process of not only generating resources but getting people together, setting up a stream into which one can put oneself, both to acquire information and training and also to test out what one has learned in the field and measure it against what other people are doing.

GORDON:

I think that every international consultant ought to belong to a professional organization in their own country and at least one international professional organization. They also ought to attend some kind of an inservice opportunity, conference or workshop at least once a year, and to refresh and renew themselves. I also feel there is a need to encourage professional schools in higher education, whether we're talking about the business schools, engineering, social work, education, or public administration, to develop in the curriculum programs that will help develop internal staff specialists and the external consultant as part of the curriculum requirements of people working in the helping professions.

RONALD:

I think another notion that needs to be implemented in any kind of cross-cultural teaming is the acceptance of the notion that in addition to the task time there needs to be seminar time, inquiry time, "looking at what we're doing" time, which can really be an essential part of the consultation project.

GORDON:

That triggers off in my mind the need for each of us to take more responsibility for "recall logs" of information, whether it's diaries, an evaluation report, whether it's writing up the report of a failure or a success, sharing it with colleagues for critique, or recording of our own experience for the value to others, that will serve as a follow-up to the project.

DAVID:

I suppose I'm suggesting something that is terribly basic and obvious, but just the simple thing of being sure to set aside some time to pursue those areas that are unfamiliar in the cross-cultural field is important. There are aspects of this field which have not come our way as consultants, because up to now there's been little built into either our experience or training.

RONALD:

Very often you may not know what those are, but if you've got a trusted colleague who knows that you're interested in finding out, he/she can be very supportive and helpful.

GORDON:

Let me mention three things about professional associations. One is that they can provide a resource of face-to-face conferencing; secondly, they could provide a resource of materials, bibliographies, and instruments that are available in cross-cultural situations; and third, they could provide some stimulus for standards of performance. I'm not sure I think that accrediting is the answer to everything, but at least the idea of developing some norms of competence that one can do some self examination about as well as ethical standards would be helpful.

DAVID:

I would add to that communication media, newsletters, publications, etc.

RONALD:

Those publications can be a linkage process for actual referrals. People who are looking for resources to be able to find others through publications.

4. How can innovations, experiences and projects be more effectively reported and shared so as to benefit the cross-cultural community as a whole?

DAVID:

One thing that we have talked about often and which in fact is slowly coming into being piece by piece is a central source of information, a data bank, a central mailing list—in short, a clearing house. It is hard to create a good clearinghouse in any field, but it may be that the need in the cross-cultural field is critical.

RONALD:

One of the typical problems of the clearinghouse is that those who are the innovative practitioners are not particularly either motivated or even competent to articulate very well the core aspects of their success or their practice. There really needs to be a notion of interviewing them as informants, and I think one of the notions of clearinghouses ought to be using some of the techniques of oral history and doing tape recording or interviewing with systematic questions, just as one would do a survey interview.

This links back to the question around acquiring competence. Think for example of those who are seeing themselves as wanting to learn or get apprenticed in the consulting area, having the job of doing interviewing, having that legitimatized as a way for them to learn, but on the other hand for them to get the data from the experienced practitioners and make it available to the field.

DAVID:

That suggests a kind of apprenticeship process, which is something to which we ought to give careful consideration. Any profession that is going to develop must offer an apprenticeship experience. It is particularly needed in this field because of the paucity of more formalized or academic training that is available .

GORDON:

I think another aspect of the storage and retrieval of data is to also

secure data from the client. I do not think we are doing a good enough job getting experience about consultations from the consumer. Therefore, we haven't been able to help the user to understand how to make most effective selection, use and evaluation of the consultant. Frequently some of the multi-national corporations, international organizations, such as World Bank, the UN, and others who do use consultants, both external and internal, could provide valuable data both from the client and the consultant point of view.
DAVID:

Another related problem is that too much of the work in the cross-cultural field has been done in the U.S. That is natural, since we obviously do communicate with ourselves more and probably better, yet at the same time, it constitutes a kind of violation of the cross-cultural principles that we are articulating.
GORDON:

What you are suggesting is very much needed. It would be interesting to get foundation grants to collect data from people providing help in the far East, Africa, and South America. They might have some new and different ways of giving help, it might open our eyes, and also to broaden our providing of help to other consultants, including technological experts, engineers and agricultural experts. We also ought to look at some of the other kinds of help givers in society, including religious consultants, community development leaders, educational specialists, etc.
RONALD:

Can't you see a kind of a conference where half the participants are the organizational leaders or users of consultants and the other half the consultants; part of the time they are working separately at skills of how to utilize consultants effectively or how to be consultants, and then they would do some practice work with each other—it would be quite a conference.

APPENDICES

A. Summary of Last Conference Session on ICF in the Future.
B. Looking at Cross-Cultural Conferencing Processes.
   by Richard D. Miller
C. Final Conference Schedule.
D. Group Leaders Guide.
E. Guides for the Group Reporter/Recorder.
F. Group Reporter/Recorder Form.
G. List of Participants.
H. Information About the International Consultants Foundation.

APPENDIX   A
SUMMARY OF LAST CONFERENCE
ON
ICF IN THE FUTURE

At the last session of the "Helping Across Cultures" conference, we took a "trip into the future of ICF". We broke up into small working teams of 3-5, went ahead two years in time and made observations of what we saw that pleased us about the activities, organization, and support of ICF which pleased us about what had come to pass.

At that session we said that at the next ICF conference we want to be able to continue the impetus of our first sessions by using the notion of trying to get some case studies in which the consultees and consultants are brought together to analyze their experience and being helped to highlight learnings and implications.

Each work group put their future images (on newsprint) up on the wall and participants read all the contributions. As they read they distributed ten votes to indicate their priorities for ICF activities, and ten votes to indicate their preferences about ICF organization. Let's look at the findings about ICF future priorities first.

ICF PROGRAM PRIORITIES

First Priority—Two to four cross-cultural consultation contracts, e.g., World Bank, UN, multi-national business, management consultation for small businessmen in Africa.

Second Priority—Several publication projects, e.g., "How to select, use, evaluate international consultants," "The consultant's role in management development in cross-cultural contexts."

Third Priority—Invitational conference of international consultants, in Europe or Asia, or two conferences a year in different parts of the world.

Fourth Priority—Information exchange center for sharing of innovations and experiences.

Fifth Priority—An invitational conference for Senior program officers— USAID, CIDA, UNDP, multi-national corporations, etc.

These were the five activities that received significant support. They certainly add up to a balanced and significant program.

Now let's look at the way the conference saw ICF developing as an organization to develop and sustain these activities.

THE STRUCTURE AND FUNCTIONING OF ICF

First Priority—The central office is making 3 referrals a month to members, they are teaming co-consultants, and they are matching consultants to client needs.

Second Priority—There are 150 members (up to 300), and less than 50% are from the USA, with members from over 50 countries.

Third Priority—There is a Client Advisory Board, meeting prior to the annual conference.

Fourth Priority—There is an elected Board, and an active Executive Committee, which has a monthly telephone conference meeting.

Fifth Priority—There is a thorough Resource Directory of member skills, interests, needs, etc.

Sixth Priority—Every 3 months members are asked to vote on, or react to, Executive Committee proposals, or state opinions on issues.

Continuation of the ICF Newsletter and Registry was assumed.

The key themes of organization seem to be mechanisms for involvement of members, active leadership, and procedures for linking members to clients.

Another way in which the subgroups made their observations was in terms of what they saw members receiving from their membership in ICF. Here is a brief tabulation of their images of the future:

MEMBERS CONTRIBUTING TO ICF

Highest frequency—Sharing their innovations, documentation for publication, writing articles, contributing, copyrights.

Second priority—Securing contracts and grants for ICF

Third priority—Recruiting new members

Fourth priority—Finding clients

Fifth priority—Task force and committee work for ICF

CONTRIBUTION TO MEMBERS FROM ICF

First priority—Exchanging methods, professional stimulation

Second priority—Receiving referrals for work and clients

Third priority—Credibility and visibility

Fourth priority—Chance to co-consult in interdisciplinary teams

So we see a theme of both giving and receiving with the emphasis on sharing and exchanging techniques and consulting experiences. A second theme emphasizes the importance of collaboration in finding clients and teaming to work with them.

HOW IS ICF FINANCED IN THE FUTURE?

This was the final topic of the two year ahead observation made by the conference participants.

Most participants seem to feel that dues could not and should not be the major source of income, but that the activity contributions of members (writing, consulting, conference leadership) could generate significant income.

This activity of "future tripping" generated a great deal of creative energy and involvement. It seemed to help the conferees move toward a readiness to commit time and energy to take steps toward achieving these images.

The concrete decision to create this book flowed from this discussion.

APPENDIX B
LOOKING AT CROSS-CULTURAL CONFERENCING PROCESSES
by
Richard D. Miller

INTRODUCTION

The evaluation process is the final element of the feedback loop which completes the conference process. It is perhaps the most difficult task in which to achieve objectivity, because of the dual roles played by most of the evaluators. That is, in addition to being an evaluator and participant, many were also planners and organizers. In spite of the caveats inherent in evaluating such a *family and workshop style* conference, the task will be undertaken in three phases.

The first phase will include providing a summary of the design and organization of the conference. Phase two will look at the results as seen by the participants during the general session evaluation. The third and final phase will examine the program from the view of the planners and the coordinator. Throughout this section one should keep in mind that the ultimate purpose of a conference evaluation is twofold: First, it should determine the degree to which the objectives, identified initially by the conference planners, were met; and second, it should determine how well participant needs were met.

CONFERENCE DESIGN

Following several preliminary discussions between Thomas Attwood and Gordon Lippitt in January 1977 an initial conference prospectus was published in February 1977. The purpose of the conference was to *bring together business managers, government leaders and key people from the helping professions to explore problems, causes and possible solutions to increasing the effectiveness of giving and receiving help in cross-cultural settings.*

The planning hypothesis was that *results today, especially in consultation from one country to another, depend more and more on people skills between helper and helpee. But, problems inevitably occur when people of different cultures intermingle. Concepts and methods which are successful in one country can spell disaster in another.*

The initial design anticipated that invitations would be extended in such a manner as to achieve the following balance in an anticipated ninety participants:

—One-third would be operating managers with experience in multi-national problems and in working with consultants.

—One-third would be internationally oriented internal consultants experienced in working with external consultants.

—Finally, one-third would be experienced cross-cultural external consultants.

To achieve the initial goals established by the preliminary planning task force a conference work plan was designed. Interim modifications and the final conference schedule are shown in Appendix C. The preliminary planning task force consisted of the following persons:

—Thomas J. Attwood, President of ICF and President of Cargill Attwood International

—Gordon L. Lippitt, Chairman of the Board of ICF and Professor of Behavioral Science at The George Washington University

—Michel Caracushansky, Director, Centro De Produtividade Do Brasil, Sao Paulo, Brasil

—Ronald Lippitt, President of Human Resources Development Associates of Ann Arbor and former professor at the University of Michigan

—Donald Swartz, President of Effectiveness Resource Group, Inc. of Tacoma, Washington.

In March, Richard D. Miller, President of R.D. Management Associates, Inc. was asked to join the group as conference coordinator and in May, Leonard Nadler, Professor of Education at The George Washington University, and President of Nadler Associates, was asked to join the planning committee.

During the early period of organizing the conference funds and participant indentification were of major interest. It was initially anticipated that each participant would contribute toward his or her own expenses and contribute to a travel fund which would assist potential participants from third-world countries which might have currency conversion difficulties. Fund raising efforts included personal, telephonic and written contacts with private and public foundations, multi-national corporations, international organizations, and several government agencies tasked with cross-cultural activities. It soon became evident that the December conference date was too soon to raise any significant level of funding through grants or corporate contributions. Organizations contacted had already established grants for the year and Government agencies uniformly were opposed to supporting such conferences outside the continental limits of the United States. In late June it was decided to conduct the conference with participant registration fees and several small grants from the Society for Intercultural Education, Training and Research (SIETAR), Organization Renewal, Inc., Project Associates, Inc. and Saga Corporation.

With the funding decision made, participant invitations were then sent out to representative groups and individuals. The following three months were spent processing registration applications and arranging conference accomodations with the Castle Harbour Hotel in Bermuda. During this period the primary planning staff of Gordon Lippitt, Richard Miller and Leonard Nadler finalized the conference program (see Appendix C). To support the final conference plan, group assignments were made. To facilitate successful group activities, group leaders and group reporters were also designated for each session. Duties of the leaders and reporters are outlined in Appendices D and E. Forms for reporting group activities were provided for each session and are shown in Appendix F.

Finally, as the last step before the actual conference, all participants were sent a letter reaffirming conference arrangements and providing helpful hints on traveling to Bermuda.

PARTICIPANT EVALUATIONS

Participant evaluation was a dynamic process which proceeded from the first evening and continued through to the end of the conference. Since the conference was relatively compact each participant had continuous access to the planners and coordinator. As participant inputs were acquired conference planners met each morning for breakfast to adjust the schedule so as to respond to participant needs in the most positive way possible. Additionally, time was made available during the afternoon of the first day to discuss participant interests for subsequent sessions. As a result the schedule was modified to allow for more time to be spent in unstructured small group settings.

The formal evaluation effort took place on the final morning when all participants were asked three questions:

I. What were the strengths of the conference in terms of outcome for you?

II. What are your ideas for revision/improvement?

III. What specific recommendations do you have for the future, i.e., future meetings?

Participants' responses to each question were as follows:

I. Strengths

1 Opportunity to meet with people who share my commitment.
2. Quality of group discussion.
3. Exposure to new techniques.
4. Diversity of experience of participants.
5. Enriched my own practice in my country for prospects of cross-cultural activities.
6. The experience of being a minority (a European's comment).
7. Chance for personal insight on issues.
8. The excitement of contact with people with wide contacts.
9. Hearing in-depth from the author of the innovations in person.
10. Validated own experiences.
11. Opportunity to share common problems.
12. Watching the emergence of an organization (ICF).
13. Development of identification with ICF.
14. Opportunity to meet socially with those I have heard about for several years.
15. The wide range of types of participants.
16. Flexibility of design.
17. Generated ideas for a specific workshop and for my own practice.
18. The conference was small enough for personal contacts.

II. Revisions

1. Less time allocated for small group reporting.
2. Need a way to reproduce small group work on-site instead of a single report at close of conference.
3. Should find a central geographic location for conference.
4. There seemed to be an over-concern for process of participation (versus committee job).
5. There needs to be more chance for participants to contribute to conference design.
6. There should be more options for establishing groups, i.e., shift membership instead of staying in assigned groups for entire conference.
7. More multi-cultural compostion and focus (more weight to minority voices).
8. Better balance in representation of client population (e.g. more

Third World participants).

9. Need more time for in-depth discussion of fewer topics.
10. Need a pre-conference response sheet by participants to suggest design.

III. Specific Recommendations

1. When asking participants to provide innovations they should be supplied a:
   a) sample of a good write-up
   b) format for write-up
   c) indication of aids available and space for indication of aids desired for presentation
2. Develop a personal profile format which can be provided by each participant (non-threatening).
3. Concurrent one hour sessions by members.
4. Combine conference and workshop methods.
5. Hold next conference in London with Per Holmlov, Tom Attwood and Bob Bhavnani as initial conference planners.
6. Continue to hold ICF conferences outside the United States.
7. Video tape ICF conference proceedings.
8. Provide space for participants to display material which they have developed.

In addition to the formal and informal evaluations discussed thus far, a third form of self or group evaluation took place during a group discussion later entitled "Underlying Assumptions Shown at the ICF Conference." During the group discussions on generalizations about helping across cultures one group had become increasingly sensitive to the cultural bias which was unconciously creeping into the behaviour of the conferees. The actions, group interpretations, and possible cross-cultural implication are shown on page 67.

It is apparent that the conference in its modified configuration met many of the felt needs of the participants. It is also apparent, however, that a very dynamic structure was required to respond to the diverse needs articulated by the twenty-eight conferees. The dynamic nature of the structure allowed the group the latitude to examine important issues such as the participant's unconcious biases which might otherwise have gone unnoticed, or at least unchallenged. This would certainly have been to the detriment of all participants.

The next step is to examine how well the conference met the goals and objectives established by the planning committee in its pre-conference deliberations.

Evaluation of Planning Committee Objectives

The ICF conferees included 28 participants (See Appendix H) and seven non-participating partners. Active participant's homes of record were as follows:

    U.S.A..............20
    Canada............ 4
    Europe............ 2 (1 former Indian)
    Latin America....1
    Bermuda.......... 1 (former Canadian)

These include nineteen males and nine females. The primary occupational breakdown was:

    Consultants   15 (53.6%)
    Academics   7 (25%)
    Government   1 (3/6%)
    Other*   5 (17.8%)

A comparison of participation ratios shows that the target of one-third internal consultants and one-third multinational business managers was not met. However, 28.6% of the participants were from non-U.S. nations and 75% of the participants were experienced cross-cultural external consultants. Departing from the purely statistical aspects of the conference evaluation, one must also look at the implied purposes. The goal of the conference was to *explore causes and possible solutions to increasing the effectiveness of giving and receiving help in cross-cultural settings.* To accomplish this goal a number of secondary (and implied) goals were established through the medium of the schedule. This included the following:

1. Identify key problems in giving and receiving help.
2. To categorize essential issues.
3. To analyze the blocks, failures, and successes in effective cross-cultural consultation.
4. To identify areas needing further research and innovation.
5. To share innovations.
6. To develop innovative projects, evaluation and future experience retrieval processes.

The degree to which the above secondary goals were accomplished can best be seen in Chapters II, III, and IV. Items 1, 2, 3, and 5 were accomplished very effectively. However, due to the schedule restructuring which was done in order to more fully respond to conferee interests, items 1, 2, 3 and 5 weren't addressed in any substantive way, but the decision to develop a book from the conference was a specific follow-up action that partially addressed the issue.

---

*Partners of participants categorized above. Many are teachers in their own right or periodically assist partners in the consulting business.

Cultural Bias Inherent in Conference Behaviour

Individual or Group's Comment or Action	Group's Interpretation	Cross-cultural Implication
1. "In this country"	*We* are "Overseas" in Bermuda	Cross-cultural implies recognition of each other's uniqueness and commoness.
2. Group reports articulate "Our group is best."	Competition assumption strong factor of U.S. culture.	Cross-cultural implies we are all partners in common in the totality of things.
3. "Big country" to "small country" for help	Assumes large is beautiful and best.	Cross-cultural implies anyone who is competent can help whatever the size or technology level.
4. Not only the "Ugly Americans"	Implication of consultants or change agents coming from the United States. Also seems to imply U.S.A. is America.	Cross-cultural implies each person must be concerned with excessive pride, arrogance and domination.
5. "How they learn in Europe"	Deductive vs. inductive.	Cross-culture suggests that we all learn in common ways.
6. Geographical choice of conference	Bermuda "lies" between U.S. and Europe	Cross-cultural implication of distance and convenience.
7. Choice of conference date	Christmas	Values of family life differ by individuals not cultures.
8. Conference design	Small groups and minimum degree of structure.	Relevant to the situation and to contemporary needs

68

APPENDIX   C

INTERNATIONAL CONSULTANTS FOUNDATION
Presents
INVITATIONAL WORLD WORK CONFERENCE
ON
HELPING ACROSS CULTURES
December 28, 29, 30, 1977
Bermuda

AGENDA

ARRIVAL DAY—December 27, 1977   **Resource Persons**

8:00-9:30 p.m.	General Session	
	Conference Welcome	Gordon Lippitt
	Conference Program	Richard Miller
	Introduction of Conferees	All participants
		and partners
9:30-10:00 p.m.	Group Leaders and	All participants
	Reporters Organization	
	Meeting	

FIRST DAY—December 28, 1977   **Resource Persons**

9:00 a.m.-12:00 noon	Identification of Key Issues in Cross-Cultural Helping (In Five Groups)	Group Leaders (as designated)
***1:30 p.m.-3:30 p.m.	International Dialogue	
4:00 p.m.-5:00 p.m.	General Session Group Reports on Key Issues	Conference Leader Don Swartz
5:00 p.m.-5:30 p.m.	Categorization and Prioritization of Issues (In Five Groups)	Group Leaders
5:30 p.m.-7:00 p.m.	Exploring the basic elements and Guidelines in Helping Across Cultures: Generalizations	Group Leaders

SECOND DAY—December 29, 1977   **Resource Persons**

9:00 a.m.-10:00 a.m.	General Session Group Reports on Generalizations	Conference Leader- Len Nadler
10:00 a.m.-12:00 noon	Reports and Discussion on Innovations sub- mitted by participants	Conference Leader- M. Caracushansky (and innovators)
***1:30 p.m.-3:30 p.m.	International Dialogue Center	
4:00 p.m.-7:00 p.m.	General Session Continued	Conference Leader- M. Caracushansky (and innovators)
	Reports and Discussions on Innovations sub- mitted by participants	

THIRD DAY—December 30, 1977   **Resource Persons**

9:00 a.m.-11:00 a.m.	Group discussions of means of creating inno- vations and identifica- tion of participant research, experiments or experiences	Group Leaders
11:00 a.m.-12:00 noon	General Session	Conference Leader- Ronald Lippitt
	Conference discussion of Action Elements Con- ference Evaluation	Rick Miller
12:00 noon	Departures	

***Between programmed sessions, participants are invited to utilize the International Dialogue Center for continued discussions with group members or other colleagues.

ICF WISHES TO ACKNOWLEDGE AND THANK THE FOLLOWING ORGANIZATIONS FOR THEIR SUPPORT AND CO-SPONSORSHIP OF THE HELPING ACROSS CULTURES CONFERENCE: Society for Intercultural Education, Training and Research (SIETAR); Saga Corporation; Project Associates, Inc.; and, Organizational Renewal, Inc.

APPENDIX D
INTERNATIONAL CONSULTANTS FOUNDATION
Presents
INVITATIONAL WORLD WORK CONFERENCE
ON
HELPING ACROSS CULTURES
Group leaders guide

Thank you for agreeing to be a group leader. In this role, your responsibilities will include both administrative and facilitative functions. Administrative functions include:

- Identifying and meeting group members (especially initial sessions).
- Guiding group members to group meeting sites designated by the conference coordinator.
- Getting group meetings started and finished on time so participants can rejoin general sessions or make other appointments in a timely fashion.
- Ensuring that group activities are organized to facilitate keeping a record of the group's deliberations, i.e. provide a method by which important points are periodically summarized.

Facilitative functions include assisting the group to focus its energies on the issues in such a way that conclusions contribute to the furtherance of session objectives. To assist you in this task, the following questions are provided as possible discussion points.

First session
9:00 a.m.—12:00 a.m. and 5:00 p.m.—5:30 p.m., December 28, 1977
1. What key issues can we isolate in providing cross-cultural help?
2. What factors contribute to the issues being concerns, blocks, or reinforcers?
3. How do the issues interfer with or reinforce the potential for helping across cultures?

Second session
5:30 p.m.—7:00 p.m., December 28, 1977

1. What are the key principles or guidelines which should guide a consultant and client in establishing a collaborative relationship in cross-cultural environment?
2. What essential competencies are required of a consultant working in a cross-cultural environment?
3. What experiences or training should a consultant obtain to work effectively in a cross-cultural environment?

Third session

9:00 a.m.—11:00 a.m., December 30, 1977

1. What is the process by which innovations are created?
   a. What are the elements of a successful innovation?
   b. What are key problems to be aware of when creating an innovation?
2. What research is currently ongoing with respect to cross-cultural assistance?
   a. What are the sources of information for ongoing research in this field?
   b. What sources of funding and/or sponsorship exist to support such research?
3. What specific experiences have participants had with respect to cross-cultural assistance? These may be in the form of lessons learned of either a positive of negative nature.

APPENDIX E

GUIDES FOR THE GROUP REPORTER/RECORDER

As the recorder/reporter, you are responsible for keeping a record of the group discussion, including agreements, disagreements and recommendations. You are a member of the leadership team, with the discussion leader.

WHAT A GROUP NEEDS FROM A RECORDER/REPORTER

— Help in keeping a record of the main points of discussion, including the facts and opinions the group considers in dealing with its problems; agreements and disagreements and final decisions or recommendations.

— Help in keeping track of topics that are mentioned but not discussed fully.

— Help in keeping track of pertinent questions or "bright ideas" that can be used later.

— Help in summarizing periodically the group's thinking and advising the group on its position in relation to its goals.

— Help in providing the concluding review and summary of the group's work.

— Help in presenting the discussion report to the total conference (if requested to do so).

Note: Please turn in your summary to Rick Miller following the session for which you are the reporter/recorder.

72

International Consultants Foundation Conference
Bermuda—December 28, 29, and 30, 1977

APPENDIX F
GROUP REPORTER/RECORDER FORM

Name of Reporter: _____ Group: _____
Session: Date: _____ Note: You might want to put an
          A.M. _____   asterisk(*) by key items
          P.M. _____   to report to total group.
                                        Please turn this form in to
                                        Rich Miller.

TOPICS DISCUSSED	OUTCOME OF DISCUSSION	NEW IDEAS

APPENDIX G
INTERNATIONAL CONSULTANTS FOUNDATION
"HELPING ACROSS CULTURES" WORK CONFERENCE
December 27, 28, 29, 30, 1977
Bermuda
List of Participants

Ishwar BHAVNANI
M.I. Corp.
Albanuss. 5
6242 Kronberg. 3
West Germany

David S. BROWN
Dept. of Public Administration
School of Government and Business
  Administration
The George Washington University
Washington, D.C. 20052

**Michel CARACUSHANSKY
CPB—Centro de Productividade do Brasil
Rua Itambe 222
Sao Paulo, Brazil 01239

Guy DARVEAU
Centre De Formation Et De Consultation
822 Sherbrooke St. East
Montreal, Quebec, Canada H2L 1K4

Robert L. HIRSH
Professional Management Corp./
  R.L. Hirsh Assoc., Ltd.
375 East Main St.
Bay Shore, New York 11706

Per H. HOLMLOV
INDEVO (The Institute for Industrial
  Evolution)
Regeringsgatan 30
Stockholm, Sweden S-111 53

David S. HOOPES
S.I.E.T.A.R.
Georgetown University
Washington, D.C. 20057

Kay HOOPES
c/o David S. Hoopes
S.I.E.T.A.R.
Georgetown University
Washington, D.C. 20057

Herman HOPLIN
1025 Santa Maria Court
McLean, Virginia 22101

R.B. KEUSCH
School of Business
East Carolina University
Greenville, North Carolina 27834

**Gordon L. LIPPITT
Chairman of the Board
International Consultants Foundation
5605 Lamar Road
Washington, D.C. 20016

Peggy LIPPITT
Human Resource Development Associates
  of Ann Arbor
1916 Cambridge Road
Ann Arbor, Michigan 48104

Phyllis LIPPITT
Project Associates, Inc.
5605 Lamar Road
Washington, D.C. 20016

**Ronald LIPPITT
Human Resource Development Associates
  of Ann Arbor
1916 Cambridge Road
Ann Arbor, Michigan 48104

Carl F. LUTZ
Consultant in Personnel Management
175 E. Delaware Place (Suite 6020)
Chicago, Illinois 60611

Beatrice MALIN
c/o Garld Malin
Dept. of Social Services
2240 Albert St.
Regina, Saskatchewan S4P 2Y2, Canada

Marian METZGER
Professional Management Corp./
  R.L. Hirsh Assoc., Ltd.

375 East Main St.
Bay Shore, New York 11706

Dorothy MILLER
R.D. Management Associates, Inc.
5597 Seminary Road (#1704)
Falls Church, Virginia 22041

*Richard D. MILLER
R.D. Management Associates, Inc.
5597 Seminary Road (#1704)
Falls Church, Virginia 22041

Kenneth L. MURRELL
KLM CONSULTING
550 W. Surf
Chicago, Illinois 60657

**Leonard NADLER
Nadler Associates
Box 536 N. College Park Station
College Park, Md. 20740

Zeace NADLER
Nadler Associates
Box 536 N. College Park Station
College Park, Md. 20740

William J. REDDIN
International Publications, Ltd.

Penthouse Suite One, Mechanics Bldg.
Church St.
Hamilton 5-31, Bermuda

Gisele RICHARDSON
Richardson Management Associates, Ltd.
4134 Dorchester Blvd. W.
Montreal, Quebec, H3Z 1V1, Canada

Marian K. SVINTH
Effectiveness Resource Group, Inc.
1611 McGilvra Blvd. East
Seattle, Washington 98112

**Donald H. SWARTZ
Effectiveness Resource Group, Inc.
6709 Topaz Drive, S.W.
Tacoma, Washington 98498

Wilson L. TILLEY
W.L. Tilley Associates
205 Merrow Road
Coventry, Conn. 06238

*   Conference Coordinator
** Program Committee

APPENDIX   H
INTERNATIONAL CONSULTANTS FOUNDATION

International Consultants Foundation,

founded in 1973 as a nonprofit organization, is a group of highly qualified consultants and development training specialists from diverse fields. Members resgistered come from over 26 countries from all continents.

Believing in people,

the Foundation recognizes the need for building on the human potential of persons, groups and organizations. For a great variety of administrative areas, the Foundation resources offer skilled conceptual assistance, apply innovative change strategies, and furnish managerial expertise and organizational evaluation capabilities.

ICF's purpose

is to bring together and utilize multinational professional consultants from the behavioral and management sciences to provide expertise for organizations worldwide.

Objectives:

1. To foster greater integration and exchange among consultants in various nations—of concepts approaches and trends in applying behavioral and management science to real problems.
2. To encourage professional and ethical standards for international consultants and those they serve.
3. To encourage, implement, and support research studies on the value of consulting practices used by consultants in various cultures.
4. To maintain a link between consultants and business, governmental, educational, research and professional institutions.
5. To develop and provide an international registry of competent resource personnel whose consulting services are available to assist in problem solving to interested persons, organizations, and international groups.
6. To secure funding for appropriate projects in assisting the development of effective management.
7. To provide resource personnel to facilitate the introduction, implementation and evaluation of efforts which help to increase the management effectiveness of individuals, groups, organizations and countries.

ICF Consultants

Membership consists of professional persons with similar ideals, standards, and objectives. As such, it is a consortium of professional and experienced practitioners as well as many internationally respected authors, researchers, and educators.

Registered Consultant Members

Members are individuals who qualify as International Consultants and are included in the ICF Registry. Selection is based upon Executive Committee review and approval of individual applications (available from the London and Washington, D.C. offices (accompanied by an initial $100 application/ registration fee (which includes first year dues.) Once approved, membership is continuous upon payment of the annual dues ($50) and provides ongoing inclusion in the Registry.

Organizational Associates

Organizations interested in and supportive of the purposes of ICF may become organizational associates for an annual contribution of $200 or more (U.S. dollars). Along with registered consultant members, organization sponsors will be listed in the ICF Registry and will receive the ICF Newsletter and other reports.

International Consultants Foundation

The ICF was created as an educational and nonprofit organization. An Executive Board guides and implements Foundation activities at international, regional, and national levels. An Executive Committee screens, reviews, and approves applications to the ICF Consultants Registry.

Chairman
Gordon L. Lippitt*
(Professor, George Washington
University, USA)

President
Thomas J. Attwood*
(Managing Director, Cargill Attwood
International, London, UK)

Register Editor
Dorothy Miller*

Executive Secretary
Elinor Conversano*

Newsletter Editor
Mary W. Roberts*

Executive Board
M.O. Akinrele
(Managing Director, Management
Systems, Nigeria)

Shyam B.L. Bharadwaj
(Senior Faculty Member, Administrative
Staff College of India, India)

I. Bhavnani
(Corp. Training Director, Minit
International, W. Germany)

Michel Caracushansky
(Director, Centro de Productividade
do Brasil)

H. Eric Frank
(Professor, University of Bath, England)

Per Holmlov
(Management Consultant, INDEVO,
Sweden)

David Hoopes*
(President, Intercultural Network,
Washington, D.C.)

Leonard Nadler*
(President, Nadler Associates, USA)

Oscar Padilla
(Ingenieros Padillay Asociados, Caracas,
Venezuela)

James G. Patton
(International Consultant, Chairman,
Patton Associates, California, USA)

Gisele Richardson
(President, Richardson Management
Associates, Montreal, Canada)

Tony Osmond Turner
(International Consultant, Australia)

Leopold Vansina
(Director, International Institute for
Organizational & Social Development
Kessel-lo, Belgium)

5605 Lamar Road
Washington, D.C. 20016
Tel.: (301) 320-4409

11/12 The Green
London W5, UK

*members of Secretariat Group